THE POETRY
OF
FLIGHT

THE POETRY

OF

FLIGHT

AN ANTHOLOGY

Edited by SELDEN RODMAN

BOOKS FOR LIBRARIES PRESS

FREEPORT, NEW YORK

Copyright, 1941, by Duell, Sloan and Pearce, Inc.
Reprinted 1969 by arrangement with Duell,
Sloan and Pearce, affiliate of Meredith Press

To

ESMOND ROMILLY

Sergeant Observer, Royal Canadian Air Force

"per ardua ad astra"

STANDARD BOOK NUMBER:
8369-6041-6

LIBRARY OF CONGRESS CATALOG CARD NUMBER:
75-76939

MANUFACTURED
BY
HALLMARK LITHOGRAPHERS, INC.
IN THE U.S.A.

Acknowledgments

For permission to use copyrighted and personal material in this book, grateful acknowledgment is made to the following authors, magazines, and publishers:

SIDNEY ALEXANDER and the PRESS OF JAMES A. DECKER
for "The Plane"

FRANCIS CHICHESTER and CHRISTY & WOOD
for an excerpt from *Seaplane Solo*

DODD, MEAD AND COMPANY
for an excerpt from *The Life of the Bee* by Maurice Maeterlinck
for "Sky Writer" by William Rose Benét from *With Wings as Eagles*
for lines from *Leonardo da Vinci* by Sigmund Freud

DOUBLEDAY, DORAN AND COMPANY
for the letter to Robert Graves from *The Letters of T. E. Lawrence,* edited by David Garnett

HARCOURT, BRACE AND COMPANY
for "Dark" from *North to the Orient* by Anne Morrow Lindbergh
for excerpts from *Air Raid* by Archibald MacLeish
for excerpts from *I'll Take the Highroad* by Wolfgang Langewiesche
for a paragraph by C. G. Jung from *Modern Man in Search of a Soul*

HOUGHTON MIFFLIN COMPANY
for the story of Pegasus from Nathaniel Hawthorne's *The Wonder Book*

ALFRED A. KNOPF
for "Mallard" from Rex Warner's *Poems*

PAYSON LOOMIS
for his translation of Alexander Blok's "The Aviator"

FLEMING MACLIESH
for "Exploration by Air," hitherto unpublished

THE MACMILLAN COMPANY
for "An Irish Airman Foresees His Death" from the *Collected Poems* of W. B. Yeats
for five stanzas of "The Frigate Pelican" from Marianne Moore's *Selected Poems*

HAROLD OBER
for excerpts from Cecil Lewis's *Sagittarius Rising*

OXFORD UNIVERSITY PRESS
for Gerard Manley Hopkins' "The Windhover" and Lauro de Bosis' *The Story of My Death*

SONIA RAIZISS and *Common Sense*
for "Message Received"

RANDOM HOUSE and THE MODERN LIBRARY
for "The Caged Eagle's Death Dream" from *Selected Poetry* by Robinson Jeffers
for excerpts from "The Orators" in *Poems* by W. H. Auden
for excerpts from *Man's Hope* by André Malraux
for the first two pages of the story "All the Dead Pilots" in William Faulkner's *These Thirteen*
for "The Pioneers" from *The Airmen* by Selden Rodman

REYNAL & HITCHCOCK
    for "The Tool" from *Wind, Sand and Stars* by Antoine
    de Saint Exupéry

STEPHEN SPENDER and *The New Statesman & Nation*
    for "To Poets and Airmen"

YALE UNIVERSITY PRESS
    for "The Structure of the Plane" from *Theory of Flight*
    by Muriel Rukeyser
    for excerpts from "Elegy on the Pilot" from *The Con-
    necticut River* by Reuel Denney

M. D. HERTER NORTON
    for his translation of Rainer Maria Rilke's "A Sonnet to
    Orpheus"

I would like here also to acknowledge my gratitude for
suggestions from Fleming MacLiesh, Sara Henderson Hay,
William A. Krauss, and Antoine de Saint Exupéry; and
especially, for her counsel and help, to Hilda, my wife.

Contents

"As for those wingy Mysteries in Divinity, and airy subtleties in Religion, which have unhing'd the brains of better heads, they never stretched the *Pia Mater* of mine. Methinks there be not impossibilities enough in Religion for an active faith; the deepest Mysteries ours contains have not only been illustrated, but maintained, by Syllogism and the rule of Reason. I love to lose myself in a mystery, to pursue my Reason to an *O altitudo!* 'Tis my solitary recreation to pose my apprehension with those involved Ænigmas and riddles of the Trinity, with Incarnation and Resurrection. I can answer all the objections of Satan and my rebellious reason with that odd resolution I learned of Tertullian, *Certum est, quia impossibile est.* I desire to exercise my faith in the difficultest point; for to credit ordinary and visible objects is not faith, but persuasion."

—SIR THOMAS BROWN

"On wings it is safe to go fast, dangerous to go slow. It is safe to be high, dangerous to be low. The more analytical and logical your mind, the more exasperating is this basic paradox of flying. Just as you cannot swim until you believe that the water will carry you, so you cannot really fly until you believe that the air isn't a nothing but has substance and mass and the power to hold you up. In the liberation of flight, up can become down. The flier must let go of his nervous hold on the ground and abandon himself to the air; he must think of himself, not as a part of the landscape, but as part of the wind that blows across it."

—WOLFGANG LANGEWIESCHE

THE POETRY
OF
FLIGHT

INTRODUCTION

The poetry of flight, unlike the poetry of the sail or the wheel, has not had time in which to develop gradually. It is being forced from us with a terrible urgency, though less than forty years have passed since the first flight. A new field of mechanical mastery has opened up; but that has happened before without appreciably broadening man's horizon or deepening his spiritual perspective. It is rather that profoundly in the consciousness of the race the idea of flight is associated with human aspiration and release from physical limitations. Now, on the very threshold of achievement, that dream becomes a nightmare threatening an awful vengeance for its perversion; and in desperation the soul of man reaches backward for the untarnished symbol of his hope.

To be sure, there has always been the bird, and the poetry of the bird, but that does not primarily concern us. We will give a few examples in which bird-flight is celebrated for its symbolism or in terms of its unapproachable excellence in the medium, and let it go at that. Our concern is for a field in which everyone who writes is a pioneer, and even a new poetry of the bird lies ahead of us.

Has it ever occurred to poets that a bird's blood has more red corpuscles per ounce than any other animal? "There is a complete separation of pure and impure blood in the bird's heart," writes Gordon Aymar in *Bird Flight*, "another departure from early reptilian life and another factor contributing to intensity and vigor of life. This high pitch to which it is tuned perhaps accounts for the richness of its song." The torpedo body of the Swift, the streamlined "high aspect ratio" wing of the Duck Hawk, the Gull so perfectly designed for gliding, the Quail and Grouse for hedge-hopping, the amphibian Penguin and the engine-crowded Humming-bird may well inspire the poets of the future to a kind of bird-poetry very different from the "Ode to the Skylark." What man-made machine will ever achieve the complex perfection of even the Goose's wing, guided by its 12,000 muscles? And how good it is for our urban, mechanical arrogance to be told by Lieutenant Commander Graham that ages before the Handley-Page with its slotted airfoils, the Eagle in its low-speed glides increased the angle of incidence by exactly similar automatic anti-stalling devices!

But if we were confined to the bird or the plane in our search for the poetry of flight, we would not have to search widely— or deeply. Fortunately there have been men in every age who considered flight possible. The gods flew, not to mention the demons, and was not man compounded of both? Quetzalcoatl, the departed blond helper of the Aztecs (who was to return later in such ironically destructive human shape) was the God of the Air. What child has not thrilled to the possibilities of the magic carpet and the enchanted Persian horse in the Arabian Nights? and was it accidental that the egg of the fabulous Roc that carried Sindbad was the symbol of something unattainable? In the Bible, we are told that "a bird of the air shall carry the voice and that which hath wings shall hear the matter," and the Voice out of the Whirlwind challenges Job:

> Canst thou bind the cluster of the Pleiades,
> Or loose the bands of Orion?

The legend of Icarus and Daedalus, provoking Ovid's tale and Breughel's great painting, achieved most lasting renown. But down through the Middle Ages we hear of Oliver, the Malmesbury Monk; Kaspar Mohr, the Flying Priest of Württemberg; and Father John Dampier, who is said to have taken off from the walls of Sterling Castle on hens' feathers without fatal consequences. "Princes of the Air," Burton called them, "those aerial devils that corrupt the air and cause plagues, thunders and fires, above and beneath the moon."

In modern times, from the genuinely scientific experiments of Leonardo da Vinci to the beginning of the nineteenth century, the legend assumes more credible shape, but hardly more so. Scientist, no less than poet and legend-maker, is thrown off the track by the Montgolfiers' balloon. Rousseau's "New Daedalus," Poe's "Balloon-Hoax" and the phantasies of Jules Verne and the early H. G. Wells are creatures of the same delusion. Even Count Zeppelin believed that man would never be able to fly well on wings because the wing-tips, unlike the extremities of the bird's pinions, would be nerveless.

Cayley and Stringfellow knew better. Otto Lilienthal and Langley and the Wright brothers knew better. It happened.

2

What was it about the idea of flight that dazzled the imagination of man? Was it merely the prospect of a greater freedom, of an unattainable swiftness of transportation and communication? Perhaps that was all. Perhaps the desire for this ultimate liberation, this imitation of immortality, was all. But the psychologists think otherwise. And the evidence, conscious and unconscious, of the poets of flight corroborates them.

If psychology and psychoanalysis were exact sciences it might be possible to interpret the symbolism of aviation very fully. Since they are not, and since, furthermore, they happen to be in their infancies, with no two schools subscribing to the same methods, we will accept their evidence as evidence and not as proof. The only extended discussion of the subject with which I am familiar occurs in Freud's monograph on Leonardo da Vinci. After tracing, plausibly enough, the connections between the great artist's recollection of a childhood erotic dream, his apparently celibate maturity, and his lifelong concern with flight, the psychologist concludes:

He probably hoped that he himself would sometime be able to fly, and we know from the wish-fulfilling dreams of people what bliss one expects from the fulfillment of this hope.

But why do so many people dream that they are able to fly? Psychoanalysis answers this question by stating that to fly or to be a bird in the dream is only a concealment of another wish, to the recognition of which one can reach by more than one linguistic or objective bridge. When an inquisitive child is told that a big bird like the stork brings the little children, when the ancients have formed the phallus winged, when the popular designation of the sexual activity of man is expressed in German by the word "to bird" (*vögeln*), when the male member is directly called *l'ucello* (bird) by the Italians, all these facts are only small fragments from a large collection which teaches us that the wish to be able to fly signifies in the dream nothing more or less than the longing for the ability of sexual accomplishment. This is an early infantile wish. When the grown-up recalls his childhood it appears to him as a happy time in which one is happy for the moment and looks to the future without any wishes; it is for this reason that he envies children. But if children themselves could inform us about it they would probably give very different reports. It seems that childhood is not that blissful Idyl into which we later distort it, that on the contrary children are lashed through the years of childhood by the wish to become big, and to imitate the grown-ups. This wish instigates all their playing. If in the course of their sexual investigation children feel that the grown-up knows something wonderful in the mysterious and yet so important realm, what they are prohibited from knowing or doing, they are seized with a violent wish to know it, and dream of it in the form of flying, or prepare this disguise of the wish for their later flying dreams. Thus aviation, which has attained its aim in our time, has also its infantile erotic roots.

By admitting that he entertained a special personal relation to the problem of flying since his childhood, Leonardo bears out what we must assume from our investigation of children of our times, namely, that his childhood investigation was directed to sexual matters. At least this one problem escaped repression and later estranged him from sexuality. From childhood, until the age of perfect intellectual maturity, this subject, slightly varied, continued to hold his interest, and it is quite possible that he was as little successful in his cherished art in the primary sexual sense as in his desires for mechanical matters; that both wishes were denied him.

It would be unfortunate to consider this suggestive passage an "explanation" of flight. Equally suggestive, no doubt, would be interpretations from the biological, social, economic, or religious points of view. Its importance and interest attaches to showing, as one instance, how deeply rooted in man is the idea of flight. So let us check this theory against the evidence of the poets and airmen—being careful not to make the mistake of generalizing that all pilots fly because they are "repressed" or that every story of the air must have a double meaning! Lawrence of Arabia, who spent the last years of his life in what he called the "monastery" of the Royal Flying Corps, and whose life seems to have been uniformly misogynous, is the closest modern analogue of Leonardo. Both men were possessed of enormous physical and intellectual vitality. Both bitterly spurned the compromises of the world of men, and, unable to accept either the formulas or the mystical experiences of religion, sought salvation in the remoteness or untarnished comradeship of the air. "In speed," wrote Lawrence in his curious *Confession of Faith,* "we hurl ourselves beyond the body. Our bodies cannot scale the heavens except in a fume of petrol. We enter it. We come."

"The airman's profession," writes Antoine de Saint Exupéry, "is one of renunciation . . . he renounces the love of women. And by renunciation he discovers his hidden god." "It was beautiful to see him," wrote Hawthorne of Pegasus, "this solitary creature whose mate had never been created." Langewiesche bears witness time and again to those experiences which every sensitive person who has flown a plane has felt: the disembodied but strong attraction between pilot and instructor, the fraternity of airmen, mechanics, and fans at an airport, the affection of a man for his ship. "Every time an airplane landed or took off you watched it the way sailors watch a woman walking by the pier." "Crack-up stories are to these men what sex jokes are to ordinary men: a way to handle stuff that is too strong to be taken straight." But Langewiesche ascribes another reason, which may or may not be analogous, to the fascination which danger has for airmen: "A man likes to test his nerve and get closer and closer and still a little closer to the edge of life."

Sensitive women who have flown describe other but related experiences. Is Anne Lindbergh, for example, groping for a pre-natal peace and security when she relates her sensations in the radio-operator's cockpit during a trans-Atlantic flight? "There were, in the first place, the oval walls of the fuselage, curving up around me in a way that was curiously comforting and secure. They seemed to surround me in a friendlier, warmer fashion than the straight inanimate walls of a room." More consciously, Muriel Rukeyser in *Theory of Flight* looks for a symbol of love that will contain the fulfillments of both personal physical union and collective revolutionary revolt:

Now we can look at our subtle jointures, study our hands,
the tools are assembled, the maps unrolled, propellers spun,

do we say *all is in readiness:*
the times approach, here is the signal shock?

Master in the plane shouts "Contact":
master on the ground: "Contact!"
    he looks up: "Now?" whispering: "Now."
    "Yes," she says. "Do."
    Say yes, people.
    Say yes.
    YES

3

The invention of the airplane by men with no interest in organized brutality or profits, was completed just in time to assist at the explosion of these forces in the first World War. Technically, the art of flight advanced enormously as a result of the bloody competition. And from 1914 until today aviation has been intimately associated with war. Modern wars are not designed to kindle the inspiration of poets; the wonder is that they have produced any poetry at all. But they have, and perhaps they will continue to, and the inspired pilots have been responsible for more than their share.

Of course the ambiguities of flight were foreseen long before the chancelleries of Europe vied with each other to reach the Wright brothers ahead of the U. S. War Department. The author of *Aerostation, or the Templar's Stratagem* (1784) ridicules the current balloon fad: "The widow Grumpus is balloon crazy and persuades her lover, an old bookseller, to make an ascent in an old Montgolfière. Scripps has great ideas . . . carrying bombs and 20-pounders in the air, supplying farmers with rain and confectioners with ice all the year round, not to mention stealing Saturn's ring for the British Museum."

H. G. Wells in *The War in the Air* (1908) gave a pretty realistic description of the aerial destruction of New York City, and a year later Kipling in *With the Night Mail* (a story which might have served as the model for Auden's *Airman's Journal*) describes conditions in the year 2000, when wars had been relegated to the scrap heap of history by an International A.B.C. "War as a paying concern ceased in 1967. The Convention of London expressly reserves to every nation the right of waging war so long as it does not interfere with the traffic *and all that implies*. . . . It is not etiquette to overcross an A.B.C. official's (flying) boat without asking permission. He is one of the body responsible for the planet's traffic. You must leave him alone. For humanity's sake don't try to be 'democratic.' "

Milton, in *Paradise Lost,* described the good and bad angels bombarding each other with explosives and uprooted mountains on the heights of heaven. And Tennyson, with more bathos and hardly more imagination two hundred years later

Heard the heavens fill with shouting, and there rained a ghastly dew
From the nations' airy navies grappling in the central blue.

But when the first air war actually started, airmen were much too busy learning to maneuver their flimsy cloth-and-wire craft to think in any such pseudo-poetic terms. It was as well. When they did come to write of their experiences years later they had the grounded leisure to recollect terror in tranquillity and to describe what they did in a language, like the folk-ballad of the Lafayette Escadrille, appropriate to a new technique:

Take the cylinders out of my kidney,
Take the scutcheon pins out of my brain,
Take the cam box from under my backbone
And assemble the engine again!

If the first World War did not produce a poet-pilot, it did produce a number of airmen capable of translating their experiences into most eloquent prose. Gabriele D'Annunzio had a genius for putting histrionic Byronism into his aerial exploits, but his poetry was behind him when the war started, and combat flying seems only to have increased the megalomania of his already unbalanced mind. It was different with the young men who flew. If there did not chance to be among them a D'Annunzio, much less an Owen or a Lawrence, nevertheless their reactions to the experience were worthy of the medium, and definitely those of a new century and a new technique. The novels of William Faulkner and Joseph Kessell, the stories of Richard Euringer and James Warner Bellah, the reports of Cecil Lewis, are tough but essentially civilized. The strain of cynicism running through them reflects the mixed motives of the warrior of 1914-18, the strain and desperation of untrained men in untested ships taking off for almost certain death. "O God— if there is a God—save my soul—if I have a soul." The pilots talked in this vein, drank heavily, and wondered whether the infantry knew what it meant "to be alone in the stabbing cold, with no one to talk to, no one to help you, nothing between you and the ground but a thin trembling fabric of cloth and wire and twenty thousand feet of emptiness"—but for all that, the love of his free, new craft and the bond between himself and his fellow craftsmen set him apart from others.

These feelings, at their best, extended far beyond the boundaries of race and nation, to include friend and foe in what Saint Exupéry was to call "the world of men." "Aviation united them," wrote Malraux, the poet-pilot of the Spanish Civil War, "as childbirth makes all women one." It led some airmen to foresee the plane, in the hands of an international police force, as the instrument which would eventually destroy its perverters and insure universal peace. Cecil Lewis, one of the few pilots to survive the devastating mortality of five years of combat-flying in the first World War (incredibly, he is reported to be in active service in the present war!) observed and reported the chivalric code common only to the flying services. "When they captured our pilots or observers they treated them with courtesy and gallantry, as I think we did them. I do not remember, except on one occasion over London in 1917, ever having any feelings of animosity against the Germans. They were simply 'the enemy'; their machines had black crosses, and it was our job to bring them down."

Is it any different in the present war? During 1939 and early 1940 the press was full of stories of the unusual code of honor adhered to by both sides; then, when the bombing of cities began and the censorship tightened up, they stopped. "In battle," the author of *Squadrons Up!* reports, "the airmen of today are hardhearted and practical. They have too many things to think of and too little time to think in, to spare precious seconds on sentiment. If a pilot's guns jammed or his ammunition ran out in *this* war, his adversary never waved to him and called, 'O.K., pal, streak home and get fixed up.' . . . War in the air had become a cold-blooded, lightning thing."

Having never heard or read of a pilot in the first World War carrying chivalry to the point of calling out "streak home and get fixed up," can one help wondering whether the *author* is the one who is showing "sentiment," and whether "precious seconds" and "hardheartedness" are really at such a premium in 1941?

4

The moral basis of the poetry of flight is in the airman's awareness of a pure medium, of a new instrument without terrestrial limitations, of a perspective of the earth seen whole. It is also, as we have remarked, in the comradeship of a calling to which is entrusted a large responsibility for good or evil. André Gide was not being sentimental when, after reading Saint Exupéry's *Night Flight* in 1931, he predicted that through aviation an oasis of heroism and personal integrity would survive the horrors of the wars of the future.

Who has flown and not felt the paradox of man's power: the perfect, self-righting balance of this delicate machine, the pitiful mark left by human hands on the vast panorama stretching below? Who has flown and not gloried in the illusions of power created by gunning the ship on the runway, clearing a section of steel fence for the first time by ten feet, slipping wingwise with ailerons and rudders opposed into the uprushing earth? Who has flown and not felt closer to nature for learning to look for the wind's least messengers? for understanding the reasons for diminishing thrust as one climbs into the atmosphere's rarity? for seeing the wonder of the sun go down as the tight blanket of darkness draws in from the compass's quarters, making the very air small and the hangars' cylindrical black mouths fade away as the roads become rivers of light?

Who has flown and not been struck by the annihilation of ugliness at even a few hundred feet? No remnant of planless poverty or obsolescence survives a short climb. Over a great city characteristic five-story roofs provide in uniform black the fine geometry of a gridiron. The wonder that light works on this formidable terrain depends on whether one is flying into or away from the sun. Flying into it, the impression is hard. Uniformity takes on an iron hue relieved only by such brilliancies as would resemble gongs or artillery fire if they could be heard. Of such are the rivers, whose collision with the setting sun is head on; the small bodies of water and the myriad tiny scintillations of pane-glass and windshield. But flying with the sun at one's back reverses the process, favoring everything with shadowed softness. Only a supreme act of intellect on such occasions can evoke the shapes of dumbbell tenements, mournful yards, irresponsible penthouses. "A glaze is put over life. The leaping hare is caught in a marble panel."

Lilienthal, before his glider crashed in 1896, thought that soaring *practised as a sport* might be "one of the most effective remedies for the conquest of those diseases of the machine which are incident to our modern culture." "We were flying," wrote Wolfgang Langewiesche more than forty years later, "for no better reason than that we needed flying for our souls; which probably shows that our souls were functioning none too well." "The machine," says Saint Exupéry, "which at first flush seems a means of isolating man from the great problems of nature, actually plunges him more deeply into them." The testimony of an ace in the first World War is the same: "The prosaic and worldly things—money, position, self-interest—out of which men build their little sand-castles of vanity, mean nothing."

Is it possible that through contact with the air poetry itself may experience a tremendous revival, a return from the Parlor of the Nineteenth Century and the Ivory Tower of the Twentieth, to its great tradition on the stage of life? It is possible. Better for poetry, and possibly even for the poet, to fall short of perfection in essaying an ambitious theme than to refine a cameo. An objective supra-personal poetry can only be written by poets with roots in the material and way of life they are celebrating. Poets who have succeeded in speaking for their time have been more than poets. Aeschylus was a soldier. Dante and Milton were statesmen. Shakespeare was an actor and stage-manager. Goethe, among many professions, was a biologist. Donne wrote his greatest poetry after he became Dean of St. Paul's. It was not until Alexander Pope that poetry became a profession; with the romantics and symbolists a hundred years later it was on the way to becoming a vice. Rimbaud, who gave up a promising career as a poet for East African trade and gun-smuggling in 1875, was the first to rebel against this ingrown preciosity. But he was too unbalanced by the tension of his conflict to go on writing.

There is none of this conflict between action and contemplation in sculpture. A good architect must know every inch of the ground before he retires to his drafting board. Painting is hard work. Even composing demands mastery—physical mastery—of one or more instruments. Is there any conceivable reason why writing, which takes in more territory than any of the other arts, should be confined to pushing a pen? Would Thomas Wolfe, if he had had any other outlet for his vast energy, have filled shelves of ledgers, not to mention his novels, with such a furious, formless outpouring?

But there are other reasons why the poet should be a specialist in something beside his poetry. A Virgil, a Dante, even a Goethe, could understand the *work* of his world as a whole. Today the world is too complex. The attempt to understand it from the "outside," purely by intuition, can only lead to confusion, to further "dissociation" in the mind of the artist. The poet must understand some part of his world well. He must be of his world in order to speak compellingly either for it or to it.

It is not suggested here that flight is the bridge to the regeneration of poetry in our time. It is merely to hazard the opinion, based on the various factors already considered, that it may be a bridge. There is no reason why a new poetry, having its point of entry in the functional, should not be approached in many other fields. Fleming MacLiesh's "Exploration by Air" is proof enough that it has been achieved in the field of flight.

But over and beyond the possible regeneration of poetry through flight or the effects of flight on poetry, we come to the figure of the airman himself as a symbol in the world of today. Who is this airman? He is a familiar of science—depending on science's most delicate calculations, confirming or rejecting its hypotheses—but no scientist. He is forever shifting and weighing the most stupendous landscapes and seascapes and skyscapes with his eye, rehearsing and balancing the most intangible forces in his hand—but is no artist. He is certainly not a legislator: lawyers are notorious at hangars: try to impress upon a "logical" mind that speed and height are the surest safety! He is the world's freest man, and yet its most dependent —depending for his very life, as even a seaman does not, on obedience to codes, care for minutest details, reaction to stimuli. Though he cannot function at all without the most formidable network of machine-shops, searchlights, pipe-lines, control-towers, directional beams and world-wide weather reports—he lives on the very margin of civilization, alone, above all this organization, in the sky.

When Lauro de Bosis, back in 1930, felt the supreme necessity of making a symbolic protest against the growing tyranny and inhumanity in the world, he instinctively selected the airplane as his instrument. He was a poet, sensationally popular with men and women, no neurotic. He did not know how to fly, he had no money to buy a plane. He learned to fly. Somehow he raised the money for a plane, and when that failed him, for another. Many volunteered to accompany him over Rome. He refused to risk any life but his own. He went by himself. He went unarmed. He did not carry a sword but a message of hope. He did not call for vengeance on the oppressors or sacrifice on the part of the oppressed. Liberation, he knew, must come from within; and sacrifice he did not ask, but gave.

Our age has heard much of material interest and of the salvation of society through envy and organized reprisal. But so far these movements from the bottom up have only succeeded in imposing a greater tyranny, a more frozen and barbarous organization, on the sufferers. An élite based upon hunger and worshipping power has brought only more hunger and heavier chains. Is it impossible that the élite of the future, if civilization has a future and if a true élite is to be born, will exercise their influence *from the top down?*—not by force, not through money, but by admiration of example: the willingness to sacrifice, the acceptance of responsibility, the authority of disinterested love? Is it possible that within the figure of the airman lies

"some secret, tremendous meaning not-yet plumbed"?

PART I

Exploration by Air

EXPLORATION BY AIR
by Fleming MacLiesh

I. *Solo: (Teterboro Airport)*

Somewhere in the division between aspiration
And the substantial reassurances of the ground
Whose familiar contacts rooted through Time
Bred in you impulse and habit and retreat—
This; in a deeper sense, your initiation.
You settle back in the cockpit, comb the seat
For the buckle of your safety-belt, alone,
Now, first and finally, to meet
And master your obtuse, apprentice stages;
To test against the horizons' undefined,
Limitless potential whose sheer blue pitch
Tempted you first a discipline of mind—
There, where none go but the birds, the myths spanned
Upon space, domain of fancy for other ages:
Air, tinted and alive, toward which
A grinning instructor waves you with his hand.

Phase of your primary training, this is no climax,
No summation. Your actual beginning,
Your point of manifest so-far-have-I-come
Is here only, and now attends the gun.
Tanks checked, the stabilizer set, prop spinning,

[21]

The exhaust phut-phut muttering from the stacks,
This is the moment big with the future, distended,
As somewhere *in* you—with unnameable consequences
And so shove home full throttle. The moment cracks
With it, the whole noon rent
Like a fabric, the grass around you blasted flat,
In one vibration start to roll; the tail
Comes up; ground-surface begins to blur, condense
Beneath you; the plane lightens, seems to sail
Suddenly, as with no noted difference,
No perceptible demarcation between "that"
And "this" in your trajectory—while you ease
The stick back—suddenly, the ground is there
Below, behind you at an angle. Before you these:
The cowling; the engine black-outlined on blue;
The prop's fine, silver circle; a dazzle of air.

And this—as you level off at five hundred feet,
Feeling in some sharp, effortless projection
How the edge of a bird's wing cuts the wind, the neat,
Definite decision; as you bank,
Turning on empty air to circle field—
Seems like the crossing of death, maybe, or—
Actually—your first woman, to proffer, yield
You infinite possibilities: extensions
Of world-discovery when you will meet
These weightless ceilings, lifted in the sun
Above you now, whose cool imperatives
Of peril, to the small pulse in your throat
Heart answers, hammering. You cut the gun—
The skimming smooth arc of turn, the swift down-float
Comes clean-as-compass-curve beneath your hand—

Confirming in you your credited endurance
And power of ascent—wheels, tail contact
Solidity, kiss, cushion, roll to rest.
On what? A promise, merely. An assurance.

II. *Ground Instruction*

You have watched the ships above you and learned something of their behavior, their life in the air. There were many names, each one with different points, new tricks: single- and multi-engined, all makes and types, with apparently endless specifications and statistics of performance.

Some, a few of these, you have by this time soloed, progressing from your first primary trainer whose simple complications seemed so bafflingly difficult, to later, more advanced models, of which some landed hot and some hung long on the ground. You have been initiated into monoplanes, biplanes, flaps, and retractible landing gear. You have learned how a fast ship, kicked over into a vertical, sticks tight in the turn and how a slow ship in a tight vertical squashes toward stalling-speed. You have learned how some come in with a shallow glide, floating to the almost inaudible motor, and how some drop suddenly, like a piano they say, but more like a coin in water: at a sharp angle; and you skim them over the ground, and they set in fast.

Many, the biggest, the fastest, you may never fly. And all—in the ceaseless developments of mathematics, draughting-room, wind-tunnel and test-hop—may change beyond your present recognition. But as on water the first rigged raft is present and perceptible in the latest steamer—as the spinal canal is basic and constant through all changes and modifications of the vertebrates—so through all evolutions of the machine, the technique, there

[23]

will remain the one common denominator, the apparent, essential constant: that all preempt the vertical.

And this, the air, has also been your schooling. Now you will know by the feel how it thins and expands in summer, losing its buoyancy, and how in winter when around the windscreen and your goggles the slipstream bites to the cheekbone, air packs, layer of densities, volatile lift. You have learned, like reefs and shifting hulls, the clouds: line squalls, cold fronts, stratus, the slaty cirrus; alto-cumulus in white plough-furrows; cumulo-nimbus piling up through the troposphere, enclosing in billowy, mountainous chimney bellowing updraughts.

You have learned the wind, the velocities of the wind, the pointed pinnacles of a city, dangerous to your foot, the water tower and the down-draught behind the hill. You have watched, for what it may tell you, the way the waves inch on a lake, smoke plumes from chimneys, and how—in the unparticularized, meadow-flat of the green wood far below you—the coursing breeze turns up the light side of the leaves in one long ripple.

You have learned the stricter awareness essential to stunting: It is nothing new to you now that you dive and pull the ship upright and hang there, in a kind of arrested ascent, while you kick full rudder and the plane vibrating in one motion like an opening fan, fans downward and around. It is nothing new to you now that you throw back your head and pick up on the unstable disc of the earth above you your point of reference, turning the ship on its back so that you hang there in the cockpit on your belt—the landscape and instruments difficult to read—in the cold blue wash of the vertical distances—until you come back on the stick to dive out, to swoop forward and down and around—or roll it on over losing no altitude, nose on horizon and the motor howling.

You have bred in yourself familiarity with compass and in-

[24]

strument, variation, deviation, drift; the map on your knee; the tables in the mathematics of navigation; the landmarks in foreign country; and the men. The men who, beyond your limited training and experience, master the air itself. The men who have turned to it to find here an experience in living beyond the intensities of drugs or drink. And there is no hunger—except that for success or a woman—which is like this hunger because here, in one particular, clearly-defined act is both symbolized and made actual the hunger to achieve. And a man who has tested it may be borne down a city street with the pouring crowd, and look up suddenly and see the droning silver belly of a plane breaking blue currents in the altitudes above him, and he can no more be kept from it than an old salt could be kept from the sea.

There are the usual conventions about fliers: the things you don't talk about, the aspects which are played down, the assumptions of modesty about exploits that is like those statues of nymphs with the hands lowered over the private places. These are the conventions which are fallen into easily, without conscious effort.

But do not suppose it is like the conservatism of a man with his neighbors, his house, and his position. Because the restraint is all there on the ground, and it is not a moral restraint, though they have morals; it is a conventional restraint and only belongs to one part of them. Beyond this, and more real, there is the air. And if they are good fliers and not just indifferences being carried off the ground in an aluminum tube which they control mechanically, then there is something that tells you, if you really look, in their eyes, and when you get into the air yourself, you will know it, if only a little.

For we are talking about a kind of existence, the newly-tenanted sky, the bird's aspect of the world to which you have by now grown used. To the groundling, the sky is a venture above him always prohibited, and the wind is a force and a motion; he sees it over the airport as the straightening wind-sock, as a shower of leaves, as spiralling dust. But as for you the wind is your step, is your stairway; and you gun the motor and streak forward into it, and with a single giant stride you are in it, climbing: the wind is a place you inhabit.

You have seen the elf-ring fires below you by moonlight in a Georgia swamp; the beaded city strung across the darkness; the schools, roads, factories and rectangular fields, varied only in color, of the Middle West against a background level as a table. You have seen the white shores of coral islands and where, over the long shoals, the green water clear as glass divides suddenly into the blue depths of the tropic sea; islands white-hot in the aquamarine calm like the colored, motionless Antilles on a travel-bureau's map. You have seen navigating steamships that you might pick up and put in your pocket, and harbors and hooting railways—and all like toys.

No garden, or walled park, or barred pleasance or enclosure labelled "No Admittance" was safe from the caprices of your eye; and to this free unrestrictable scrutiny by the moving mind the exploration of terrestrial details is but a gauge, an index, to the future exploration of your thoughts. At your decision the cloud-layer above you spotted with holes where the blue patch fades like a promise, like a closing scene, like a century ending in shadows—is your gate. You may climb toward it until you might reach your arm out of the cockpit and catch cloud by handfuls, cloud into which at split-second you disappear. To emerge in a new world, into dazzling, immortal blue where the sun fixes under you a snowy, illimitable undulation. Here there is no shape, no other plane, only this. You are alone, as it might be, with the clarity of your death. Under that delicate and deceptive floor of clouds is hidden—thousands of feet down—the staleness of towns. There signs flash, voices blare, men crowd doorways. Here, without knowing, you confront yourself. You have many positions. You may dive into the cloud and scoop it over you like a blank, like a moment's suspense—to blast out of it soaring upward in a loop and at the top of it hang there above those pinnacles like a mystery of rocks, until with an oriented effort of rudder and stick—as sure and decisive as the reassertion of balance—you roll out, fly on, pursue the inner conviction that it is the hidden towns there which are dying, without awareness, in a petrifaction of objects: that here the blue altitudes you travel grant an essential life.

And this, maybe, is the gist of it. For here, over a new earth, with a layer of air anywhere from 50 to 15,000 feet deep between it and the soles of your feet, as space and time telescope in speed from a third angle, the midnight provinces of Euclid where his brain wrestled are aerial performances of your blood and bone; into these you enter without formulation, without articulate understanding, with only the borderline intuition that somewhere, at the barrier of some dimension, you have broken through. And these diagrams, this easy access and traversal in symmetries and curves and configurations conceived and executed upon the upper air, hold—to that intuition, for the superconscious, for the unformed, final word trembling there in your longest memory, in your future, almost but not quite spoken —some secret, tremendous meaning not-yet plumbed.

III. *Airman's Certificate—No. 39289—U. S. Civil Aeronautics Authority*

Here to your testing, polished in the sun
With power of speeds and heights, this low-wing monoplane
Signifies a new method of perception,

Presenting to the actuary brain
In rudder, motor, elevators, ailerons,
Organic functions into which you grow
And fit yourself, the way a stumbling child
Discovers legs. Behind you the early shadow
Darkens the hangar-mouths, above you piled
Cool, cloudless immobilities. So you settle
Clumsy with chute into the seat, and someone—
The switch clicked on, the air-intended metal
Throbbing to engine—steps back, points you free,
Yelling, "It's yours!" And it begins to roll,
Picks up momentum, to whose urgency
Deep as the impatience of your soul
Racing beside you the sky's empty cup
Is held. The motor's intermittent cough,
To slight, constricted doubt, as you go up,
Melts into a tireless thunder; you level off
And in the flat trajectory of a bullet,
Barely above ground, reap to your controls
And bind and gather in, like gathering Time,
Speed which is power here; and so you pull it
Steeply against the air's-wall up; and climb.

And this is your latest element, your new locus
In temporal existence. Below you, plain,
Earth at three thousand feet in a wide focus
Preserves particulars; here you maintain
Safe distance above it—which, from your first fear,
Is now a reassurance; here you may dive
Or whirl into a spin and come out clear
With ample altitude; here you will shrive

Your sterile discursions as with wanton grace,
Bearing you like a girl, the atmosphere
Spreads itself to you now. This is your place.

This is the act men dreamed but did not know
By living counterpart. In this you meet
The turbulent angels of Michelangelo
Hurrying upward, spurning with their feet
The contours of the wind; the chariot sun,
Faust in the chowder current, the Arab Prince,
The helmeted image on revolving distance
Glittering by Chimaera, Bellerophon.
These are the figures in your Saturn-ring
Held as you bank in vertical, that flash by
Broken as you reverse it, roll to fling
Whorls and spirals out across the sky.
This is the field on which you leave no mark.
This is the singer crying to the lark.
Here in your blood, the pulse, the rolling drum:
The poet singing of Byzantium.

Here, as you flatten out your dive and zoom—
All that labor spent night after night
By Leonardo in his tower room
Manipulating bird-like, bat-like kite
Could have prefigured you attest in flight.
The demonstrations of mind's calculus
Proved to the thought but unproved to the blood
Are acted here. The hawk without a hood
Flies where, on the luminous courts you keep,
Epochs fixed their eyes, old Daedalus
Being legend to them only, except in sleep.

Your dangerous freedom, by this conquest pinned
On instabilities, voice would cry aloud
Mounting the sudden updraught—to stand on wind
Bucking beneath your feet—to soar
Into the blind, white emptiness of cloud
Riding invisibilities, then pour
The juice on into her and dive—split space,
And slowly pull the stick back, feel
Your feet press up the inside of a wheel:
And earth turns over—rolling as you race
Plane's belly to the sun above that silence
Of towery magic, with-no-foothold islands,
Whose whole soft archipelago roars to dissolve
In clear, blue immobilities as you revolve.
Until, at last, upon the height you ride
In all things reproduced and magnified,
Sky-discoverer, grow aware
Of penetrable, abstract, blue
Amazement of air.

After, when you come in and land, reflect
How long man may have mastered wheel and sail
Before those symbols caught the intellect
Which turned them to deeper meanings. Here in detail
What waits—here in man's flight what solemn speech
Forms on the future's tongue and will discover
A sense beyond the physical forms that reach
These altitudes—the woman and her lover.
What magnitudes may thought explore
Of being, which casts in this as on a screen
Its undeclared dimensions! O you—before
You damn the age—remember this machine.

PART II

The Act Men Dreamed

The Fall of Icarus
by Ovid (Golding's Translation)

Now in this while gan *Daedalus* a wearinesse to take
Of living like a banisht man and prisoner such a time
In *Crete,* and longèd in his heart to see his native clime.
But Seas enclosèd him as if he had in prison be.
Then thought he: though both Sea and land King *Minos* stop
    fro me,
I am assurde he cannot stop the Aire and open Skie:
To make my passage that way then my cunning will I trie,
Although that *Minos* like a Lord held all the world beside:
Yet doth the Aire from *Minos* yoke for all men free abide.
This sed: to uncoth Arts he bent the force of all his wits
To alter natures course by craft. And orderly he knits
A rowe of fethers one by one, beginning with the short,
And overmatching still eche quill with one of longer sort,
That on the shoring of a hill a man would thinke them grow.
Even so the countrie Organpipes of Oten reedes in row
Eche higher than another rise. Then fastned he with Flax
The middle quilles, and joynèd in the lowest sort with Wax,
And when he thus had finisht them, a little he them bent
In compasse, that the verie Birdes they full might represent.
There stoode me by him *Icarus* his sonne a pretie Lad:
Who knowing not that he in handes his owne destruction had,
With smiling mouth did one while blow the fethers to and fro
Which in the Aire on wings of Birds did flask not long ago:

[33]

And with his thumbes another while he chafes the yelow Wax
And lets his fathers wondrous worke with childish toyes and
    knax.
Assoone as that the worke was done, the workman by and by
Did peyse his bodie on his wings, and in the Aire on hie
Hung wavering: and did teach his sonne how he should also flie.
I warne thee (quoth he) *Icarus* a middle race to keepe.
For if thou hold to low a gate, the dankenesse of the deepe
Will overlade thy wings with wet. And if thou mount to hie,
The Sunne will sindge them. Therefore see betweene them both
    thou flie.
I bid thee not behold the Starre Boötes in the Skie,
Nor looke upon the bigger Beare to make thy course thereby,
Nor yet on *Órions* naked sword. But ever have an eie
To keepe the race that I doe keepe, and I will guide thee right.
In giving counsell to his sonne to order well his flight,
He fastned to his shoulders twaine a paire of uncoth wings,
And as he was in doing it and warning him of things,
His agèd cheekes were wet, his handes did quake, in fine he gave
His sonne a kisse the last that he alive should ever have.
And then he mounting up aloft before him tooke his way
Right fearfull for his followers sake: as is the Bird the day
That first she tolleth from hir nest among the braunches hie
Hir tender yong ones in the Aire to teach them for to flie.
So heartens he his little sonne to follow teaching him
A hurtfull Art. His owne two wings he waveth verie trim,
And looketh backward still upon his sonnes. The fishermen
Then standing angling by the Sea, and Shepeherdes leaning then
On sheepehookes, and the Ploughmen on the handles of their
    Plough,
Beholding them, amazed were: and thought that they that
    through

The Aire could flie were Gods. And now did on their left side
    stand
The Iles of *Paros* and of *Dele* and *Samos,* Junos land:
And on their right, *Lebinthos,* and the faire *Calydna* fraught
With store of honie: when the Boy a frolicke courage caught
To flie at randon. Whereupon forsaking quight his guide,
Of fond desire to flie to Heaven, above his boundes he stide.
And there the nerenesse of the Sunne which burnd more hote
    aloft,
Did make the Wax (with which his wings were glewèd) lithe
    and soft.
Assoone as that the Wax was molt, his naked armes he shakes,
And wanting wherewithall to wave, no helpe of Aire he takes.
But calling on his father loud he drownèd in the wave:
And by this chaunce of his, those Seas his name for ever have.
His wretched Father (but as then no father) cride in feare
O Icarus O Icarus where art thou? tell me where
That I may finde thee *Icarus.* He saw the fethers swim
Upon the waves, and curst his Art that so had spighted him.
At last he tooke his bodie up and laid it in a grave,
And to the Ile the name of him then buried in it gave.

PEGASUS
by Nathaniel Hawthorne

Nearer and nearer came the aerial wonder, flying in great circles, as you may have seen a dove when about to alight. Downward came Pegasus, in those wide, sweeping circles, which grew narrower still, as he gradually approached the earth. The nigher the view of him, the more beautiful he was, and the more marvellous the sweep of his silvery wings. At last, with so light a pressure as hardly to bend the grass about the fountain, or imprint a hoof-tramp in the sand of its margin, he alighted, and, stooping his wild head, began to drink. He drew in the water, with long and pleasant sighs, and tranquil pauses of enjoyment; and then another draught, and another, and another. For, nowhere in the world, or up among the clouds, did Pegasus love any water as he loved this of Pirene. And when his thirst was slaked, he cropped a few of the honey-blossoms of the clover, delicately tasting them, but not caring to make a hearty meal, because the herbage, just beneath the clouds, on the lofty sides of Mount Helicon, suited his palate better than this ordinary grass.

After thus drinking to his heart's content, and in his dainty fashion, condescending to take a little food, the winged horse began to caper to and fro, and dance as it were, out of mere idleness and sport. There never was a more playful creature made than this very Pegasus. So there he frisked, in a way that it delights me to think about, fluttering his great wings as lightly as ever did a linnet, and running little races, half on earth and half in air, and which I know not whether to call a flight or a gallop. When a creature is perfectly able to fly, he sometimes chooses to run, just for the pastime of the thing; and so did Pegasus, although it cost him some little trouble to keep his hoofs so near the ground. Bellerophon, meanwhile, holding the child's hand, peeped forth from the shrubbery, and thought that never was any sight so beautiful as this, nor ever a horse's eyes so wild and spirited as those of Pegasus. It seemed a sin to think of bridling him and riding on his back.

Once or twice, Pegasus stopped, and snuffed the air, pricking up his ears, tossing his head and turning it on all sides, as if he partly suspected some mischief or other. Seeing nothing, however, and hearing no sound, he soon began his antics again.

At length,—not that he was weary, but only idle and luxurious,—Pegasus folded his wings, and lay down on the soft green turf. But, being too full of aerial life to remain quiet for many moments together, he soon rolled over on his back, with his four slender legs in the air. It was beautiful to see him, this one solitary creature, whose mate had never been created, but who needed no companion, and, living a great many hundred years, was as happy as the centuries were long. The more he did such things as mortal horses are accustomed to do, the less earthly and the more wonderful he seemed. Bellerophon and the child almost held their breath, partly from a delightful awe, but still more because they dreaded lest the slightest stir or murmur should send him up, with the speed of an arrow-flight, into the farthest blue of the sky.

Finally, when he had had enough of rolling over and over, Pegasus turned himself about, and, indolently, like any other horse, put out his forelegs, in order to rise from the ground;

and Bellerophon, who had guessed that he would do so, darted suddenly from the thicket, and leaped astride of his back.

Yes, there he sat, on the back of the winged horse!

But what a bound did Pegasus make, when, for the first time, he felt the weight of a mortal man upon his loins! A bound, indeed! Before he had time to draw a breath, Bellerophon found himself five hundred feet aloft, and still shooting upward, while the winged horse snorted and trembled with terror and anger. Upward he went, up, up, up, until he plunged into the cold misty bosom of a cloud, at which, only a little while before, Bellerophon had been gazing, and fancying it a very pleasant spot. Then again, out of the heart of the cloud, Pegasus shot down like a thunderbolt, as if he meant to dash both himself and his rider headlong against a rock. Then he went through about a thousand of the wildest caprioles that had ever been performed either by a bird or a horse.

I cannot tell you half that he did. He skimmed straight forward, and sideways, and backward. He reared himself erect, with his forelegs on a wreath of mist, and his hind legs on nothing at all. He flung out his heels behind, and put down his head between his legs, with his wings pointing right upward. At about two miles' height above the earth, he turned a somerset, so that Bellerophon's heels were where his head should have been, and he seemed to look down into the sky, instead of up. He twisted his head about, and, looking Bellerophon in the face, with fire flashing from his eyes, made a terrible attempt to bite him. He fluttered his pinions so wildly that one of the silver feathers was shaken out, and floating earthward, was picked up by the child, who kept it as long as he lived, in memory of Pegasus and Bellerophon.

But the latter (who, as you may judge, was as good a horseman as ever galloped) had been watching his opportunity, and at last clapped the golden bit of the enchanted bridle between the winged steed's jaws. No sooner was this done, than Pegasus became as manageable as if he had taken food, all his life, out of Bellerophon's hand. To speak what I really feel, it was almost a sadness to see so wild a creature grow suddenly so tame. And Pegasus seemed to feel it so, likewise. He looked round to Bellerophon, with the tears in his beautiful eyes, instead of the fire that so recently flashed from them. But when Bellerophon patted his head, and spoke a few authoritative, yet kind and soothing words, another look came into the eyes of Pegasus; for he was glad at heart, after so many lonely centuries, to have found a companion and a master.

Thus it always is with winged horses, and with all such wild and solitary creatures. If you can catch and overcome them, it is the surest way to win their love.

A Sonnet

by Philippe Desportes (1546-1606)

Icare est cheut icy, le jeune audacieux,
Qui pour voler au ciel eut assez de courage:
Icy tomba sons corps degarny de plumage,
Laissant tous braves coeurs de sa cheute envieux.
O bien-heureux travail d'un, esprit glorieux,
Qui tire un si grand gain d'un si petit dommage!
O bien-heureux malheur plein de tant d'avantage,

Qu'il rende le vaincu des ans victorieux!
Un chemin si nouveau n'estonna sa jeunesse,
Le pouvoir lui faillit, mais non la hardiesse:
Il eut pour le bruler des astres le plus beau;
Il mourut poursuivant une haute adventure;
Le ciel fust son desir, la mer sa sepulture:
Est-il plus beau dessein ou plus riche tombeau?

Icarus is fallen here, the marvelous boy
Who challenged heaven with his wings; the wave
Received his body, feathers could destroy,
But left with envy in their hearts the brave.
Wondrous accomplishment, glory without end,
To pluck such honor with such dearth of tears!
Happy misfortune, that could thus extend

Victory to the conquered down the years!
Will (for a path so perilous) he did not lack,
Power eluded him, not bravery;
Stars in their flaming orbits watched his track
And marked for high adventure this wingèd doom:
The sky was his desire, his sepulchre the sea;
Is there a lovelier pattern, a richer tomb?

A Letter from Switzerland
by Johann Wolfgang von Goethe

That there are in man many intellectual capacities which in this life he is unable to develop, which, therefore, point to a better future and to a more harmonious state of existence—on this point we are both agreed. But, further than this, I cannot give up that other fancy of mine, even though, on account of it, you may again call me, as you have so often done already, a mere enthusiast. For my part, I do think that man feels conscious, also, of corporeal qualities of whose mature expansion he can have no hope in this life. This, most assuredly, is the case with *flying*. How strongly, at one time, did the clouds, driving along the blue sky, tempt me to travel with them to foreign lands! and now in what danger do I stand lest they should carry me away with them from the mountain-peak as they sweep violently by! What desire I feel to throw myself into the boundless regions of the air, to poise over the terrific abyss, or to alight on some otherwise inaccessible rock! With what a longing do I draw deeper and deeper breath, when in the dark blue depth beneath me, the eagle soars over rocks and forests, or, in company and in sweet concord with his mate, wheels in wide circles round the eyry to which he has entrusted his young! Must I, then, never do more than creep up to the summits? Must I always go on clinging to the highest rocks, as well as to the lowest plain? and when I have, at last, with much toil, reached the desired eminence, must I still anxiously grasp at every holding-place, shudder at the thought of return, and tremble at the chance of a fall?

ECSTASIS
by C. G. Jung

Among many cases, I have been especially impressed with one that concerns a colleague of mine in Zürich. He was a man somewhat older than myself whom I saw from time to time, and who always teased me on these occasions about my interest in dream-interpretation. I met him one day in the street and he called out to me: "How are things going? Are you still interpreting dreams? By the way, I've had another idiotic dream. Does it mean something too?" He had dreamed as follows: "I am climbing a high mountain, over steep, snow-covered slopes. I mount higher and higher—it is marvelous weather. The higher I climb the better I feel. I think: 'If only I could go on climbing like this for ever!' When I reach the summit my happiness and elation are so strong that I feel I could mount right up into space. And I discover that I can actually do this. I go on climbing on empty air. I awake in a real ecstasy." When he had told me his dream, I said: "My dear man, I know you can't give up mountaineering, but let me implore you not to go alone from now on. When you go, take two guides, and you must promise on your word of honor to follow their directions." "Incorrigible!" he replied, laughing, and said good-bye. I never saw him again. Two months later came the first blow. When out alone, he was buried by an avalanche, but was dug out in the nick of time by a military patrol which happened to come along. Three months after this the end came. He went on a climb, accompanied by a younger friend, but without guides. An alpinist standing below saw him literally step out into the air as he was letting himself down a rock wall. He fell onto the head of his friend, who was waiting beneath him, and both were dashed to pieces far below. That was *ecstasis* in the full meaning of the word.

The Flight of Satan
by John Milton

Mean while the Adversary of God and Man,
Satan with thoughts inflam'd of highest design,
Puts on swift wings, and toward the Gates of Hell
Explores his solitary flight: som times
He scours the right hand coast, som times the left,
Now shaves with level wing the deep, then soares
Up to the fiery concave touring high.

But glad that now his Sea should find a shore,
With fresh alacritie and force renew'd
Springs upward like a Pyramid of fire
Into the wilde Expanse, and through the shock
Of fighting Elements, on all sides round
Environ'd wins his way; harder beset
And more endanger'd, then when *Argo* pass'd
Through *Bosporus* betwixt the justling Rocks:
Or when *Ulysses* on the Larbord shunnd
Charybdis, and by th' other whirlpool steard.
So he with difficulty and labour hard
Mov'd on, with difficulty and labour hee;
But hee once past, soon after when man fell,
Strange alteration! Sin and Death amain
Following his track, such was the will of Heav'n,
Pav'd after him a broad and beat'n way

Over the dark Abyss, whose boiling Gulf
Tamely endur'd a Bridge of wondrous length
From Hell continu'd reaching th' utmost Orbe
Of this frail World; by which the Spirits perverse
With easie intercourse pass to and fro
To tempt or punish mortals, except whom
God and good Angels guard by special grace.
But now at last the sacred influence
Of light appears, and from the walls of Heav'n
Shoots farr into the bosom of dim Night
A glimmering dawn; here Nature first begins
Her fardest verge, and *Chaos* to retire
As from her outmost works a brok'n foe
With tumult less and with less hostile din,
That *Satan* with less toil, and now with ease
Wafts on the calmer wave by dubious light
And like a weather-beaten Vessel holds
Gladly the Port, though Shrouds and Tackle torn;
Or in the emptier waste, resembling Air,
Weighs his spread wings, at leasure to behold
Farr off th' Empyreal Heav'n, extended wide
In circuit, undetermind square or round,
With Opal Towrs and Battlements adorn'd
Of living Saphire, once his native Seat;
And fast by hanging in a golden Chain
This pendant world, in bigness as a Starr
Of smallest Magnitude close by the Moon.
Thither full fraught with mischievous revenge,
Accurst, and in a cursed hour he hies.

PART III

Where None Go But the Birds

Fragments from the Old Masters

The Temple-haunting Martlet

This guest of summer,
The temple-haunting Martlet, does approve,
By his loved masonry, that Heaven's breath
Smells wooingly here. No jutting frieze,
Buttress or coignes of 'vantage, but this bird
Hath made his pendent bed and procreant cradle:
Where they most breed and haunt, I have observed
The air is delicate.   —WILLIAM SHAKESPEARE

Formation Flight

Part more wise
In common, ranged in future, wedge their way
Intelligent of seasons, and set forth
Their airy caravan, high over seas
Flying, and over lands, with mutual wing
Easing their flight. So steers the prudent Crane
Her annual voyage, borne on winds. The air
Floats as they pass, fann'd by unnumber'd wings.
   —JOHN MILTON

Immortal Tent

The sky is an immortal Tent built by the Sons of Los;
And every Space that a man views around his dwelling-place,
Standing on his own roof, or in his garden on a mount
Of twenty-five cubits in height, such Space is his Universe:
And on its verge the Sun rises and sets, the Clouds bow
To meet the flat Earth and the Sea in such an order'd Space;
The Starry Heavens reach no further, but here bend and set
On all sides, and the two Poles turn on their valves of gold,
And if he move his dwelling-place, his Heavens also move
Where'er he goes, and all his neighborhood bewail his loss.
Such are the Spaces called Earth, and such its dimensions.

—WILLIAM BLAKE

The Cloud

I am the daughter of Earth and Water,
   And the nursling of the Sky;
I pass through the pores of the ocean and shores:
   I change but I cannot die;
For after the rain when with never a stain
   The pavilion of Heaven is bare,
And the winds and sunbeams with their convex gleams
   Build up the blue dome of air,
I silently laugh at my own cenotaph,
   And out of the caverns of rain,
Like a child from the womb, like a ghost from the tomb
   I arise and unbuild it again.

—PERCY BYSSHE SHELLEY

The Eagle

He clasps the crag with crooked hands;
Close to the sun in lonely lands,
Ring'd with the azure world, he stands.

The wrinkled sea beneath him crawls;
He watches from his mountain walls,
And like a thunderbolt he falls.

—ALFRED, LORD TENNYSON

To the Man-of-War Bird
by Walt Whitman

Thou who hast slept all night upon the storm,
Waking renew'd on thy prodigious pinions,
(Burst the wild storm? above it thou ascended'st,
And rested on the sky, thy slave that cradled thee,)
Now a blue point, far, far in heaven floating,
As to the light emerging here on deck I watch thee,
(Myself a speck, a point on the world's floating vast.)
Far, far at sea,
After the night's fierce drifts have strewn the shore with wrecks,
With re-appearing day as now so happy and serene,
The rosy and elastic dawn, the flashing sun,
The limpid spread of air cerulean,
Thou also re-appearest.

Thou born to match the gale, (thou art all wings,)
To cope with heaven and earth and sea and hurricane,
Thou ship of air that never furl'st thy sails,
Days, even weeks untired and onward, through spaces, realms
    gyrating,
At dusk that look'st on Senegal, at morn America,
That sport'st amid the lightning-flash and thunder-cloud,
In them, in thy experiences, had'st thou my soul,
What joys! what joys were thine!

THE WINDHOVER
To Christ our Lord
by Gerard Manley Hopkins

I caught this morning morning's minion, kingdom of daylight's
    dauphin, dapple-dawn-drawn Falcon, in his riding
Of the rolling level underneath him steady air, and striding
High there, how he rung upon the rein of a wimpling wing
In his ecstasy! then off, off forth on swing,
As a skate's heel sweeps smooth on a bow-bend: the hurl and
    gliding
Rebuffed the big wind. My heart in hiding
Stirred for a bird,—the achieve of, the mastery of the thing!

Brute beauty and valour and act, oh, air, pride, plume, here
Buckle! AND the fire that breaks from thee then, a billion
Times told lovelier, more dangerous, O my chevalier!

No wonder of it: shéer plód makes plough down sillion
Shine, and blue-bleak embers, ah my dear,
Fall, gall themselves, and gash gold-vermilion.

KNAPSACK OF SALVATION
by Wolfgang Langewiesche

When a pilot does too much flying, or flying which is more risky than suits him, or if he flies ships which are too hot for his piloting ability, something in him tires and he can no longer look at all the dangers in a cool and hypothetical fashion. Instead, he starts looking the other way; in that case he is bound to run into a whole string of troubles: mishaps, scares, crack-ups; he also is likely to talk a lot about luck without actually quite trusting it; and to drink a lot; for he knows the air is not to be fooled with. Or else he begins really to *mean* it, as it were. Instead of merely keeping in mind that the engine might quit, he thinks it really will; instead of merely keeping a couple of navigational emergency exits open in case his intended airport should fog in, he thinks it probably is fogged in already. Then in order to keep on flying, he tries to suppress his fears; and after a while, his nerves revolt.

My own case was mild—as all my flying has been mild; I am, as I have said elsewhere, no big-time flier, but just an ordinary person who likes to take an airplane up once in a while. I wouldn't even have noticed it if I hadn't been so interested in all sides of flying, even the nervous one, and I wouldn't report it if I didn't think it interesting as a miniature sketch of the real thing.

I lost confidence in the power of flowing air which is what holds an airplane up. In dreams, I often had the feeling that I was stalling—that unmistakable feeling that you get when you slow up an airplane beyond the critical point. When the wings lose their grip on the air and begin to feel like legs that have gone to sleep, numb and useless, and then they buckle—not actually, but it feels as if they did, and the ship falls off forward and unless there is altitude below you, it falls onto the ground.

Another dream involved the code in which weather reports come in over the teletype. In this dream I was returning from a cross-country flight but was unable to land because of:

Light rain—moderate rain—heavy rain—light snow—moderate snow—heavy snow—light freezing rain—moderate freezing rain —sprinkling—light mist—heavy mist—light fog—moderate fog —dense fog—light ground fog—moderate ground fog—dense ground fog—hazy—thick haze—smoky—thick smoky—dusty— thick dust—blowing snow—thick blowing snow—blowing dust— thick blowing dust—blowing sand—thick blowing sand—light ice fog—moderate ice fog—dense ice fog—light freezing mist— heavy freezing mist—light sleet—moderate sleet—heavy sleet— light hail—moderate hail—heavy hail—mild thunderstorm—moderate thunderstorm—severe thunderstorm—hurricane.

In automobiles I had some sense of relief, and sometimes I actually thought the way to travel might be on wheels, after all. In a car, control seems so steel-hard and positive, and you could slow down with never any fear that she might drop out from under you.

I felt unreasonable annoyance at the smell of motor exhaust, even if it was only an automobile's; or the sound of airplanes, even if they were only airliners which didn't concern me.

The same with heights. Heights made me feel listless and sad, even quite modest ones. I remember walking in the park with some girl and all of a sudden turning gloomy, merely—I discovered afterwards, upon thinking about it—because she chose a path which crossed a stream on a high-slung Japanese garden bridge.

But the oddest thing was that it made me uncomfortable to see any object fall; even a ball. Walking across the campus, I once saw a fellow throw a raincoat out of a fourth floor dormitory window, down to another fellow on the lawn. That seemed to me an act of utmost barbaric crudeness and a personal threat; for the arms of the coat were flapping and it looked altogether too much like a human body coming down.

I decided to do something about it.

First, following one set of advisers, I took a couple of weeks' rest from flying and the Airport. Then, following the other set of advisers, I took a delayed-opening parachute jump.

My old friends, Miller and Johnson, prepared the parachutes. But of my intention to delay the pulling of the ripcord, I did not dare tell them. I was a bit awed by it myself.

Though this was to be my second jump, it came harder than the first one; curiosity was gone, but all the worries were still left. Would I get clear the ship, or lose my nerve and pull right away, and catch in the tail surfaces? Would the 'chute, in opening after a long delay, tangle with my feet? Or would the harness tear under the opening shock? I now had much respect for the landing itself; I thought of all the places where I might land; pointed and sharp ones, or perhaps live wires, or the river. Least reasonable worry and yet uppermost: Would the 'chute open properly? And if it didn't, how much time would there be to think, and what would I think?

When I reported on the appointed day, Johnson was out. Miller had my equipment still on the workbench, where he was checking it for the last time.

His assistant was frying hamburgers for lunch. The heat was good, and so was the smell. Outside, it was late autumn. The ceiling was four thousand feet, a solid overcast; the wind was N.E. 12, and it was chilly. Not an inviting day to go falling through the sky.

Was I asking for trouble?

Miller himself had given up jumping years ago. He now spent his life firmly on the ground, servicing other people's parachutes, trading in parachutes, patching and cleaning and folding parachutes; a tailor instead of an airman. What was his final judgment on parachutes?

"How often, would you guess, can a man jump before it will get him?"

To that type of question most flying men have two answers. One answer is that everything is now under full control, that we have now achieved full mastery of the air. That is the answer you give to cash customers. The other you give to yourself sometimes, and always to the girl you want to impress:

"It is all a chance. When she is ready to hit, she will hit."

But the rigger, wise old bird, had a different point of view. Even parachute jumping, he said, was all right and reasonably safe nowadays, provided you kept your wits about you, and used only good 'chutes packed by reputable riggers like himself— after all he charged only three dollars for a re-packing job—and as long as you observed the law that two 'chutes must be worn on intentional jumps. But the trouble with the parachute-jumping public, as he put it, was that they became used to it and became careless and sloppy. "Then," he added, "it is sure to kill fast."

He snapped and tested one after another the rubber cords that were to tear open the canvas bag and spill out the silk, once the latch was ripped out.

"And don't fool yourself," he said, "that you are an exception and will remain careful; because you won't."

He was right about that in a way. Instead of a straight bailing-out, I wanted to make this a delayed-opening jump. The idea is to let yourself fall, hand on ripcord ring, for a thousand feet or so, and only then to rip. It wouldn't have taken much to discourage me, on this cool, gray morning, but I didn't want to be discouraged. So I put it to him gently. I said I had arranged this time to be dumped from a little higher up, because I wanted to hold it a little longer, and that might be easier to do with a little more altitude below.

"All right," he said, somewhat to my surprise. As a matter of fact, and quite frankly, last time I had pulled too damned soon, and it might be wise to learn to hold it a little longer. From below it had looked as if my 'chute had just barely cleared the ship's tail.

I knew that. Last time I had ripped not when it seemed best but when my nerves had ripped—at the exact moment when the fear of tangling in the tail had been overpowered by the horror and confusion of the bottomless drop. This time, I must try for absolute nerve control.

The rigger put the finishing touch to his job. With indelible ink he signed his name and the date on a white cloth label sewn to the pack. This is a licensed rigger's guarantee that a parachute has been opened, inspected, refolded, and repacked within sixty days preceding flight, as the law demands; that it will work. Then he handed it to me for my inspection. I handed it back, and he cracked the standard joke of the occasion:

"If it doesn't work, bring it back and we'll refund your money."

Miller phoned to town for the pilot to come out: this guy was here now and wanted to jump. The mechanics still had considerable fixing to do on the old biplane and its World War engine before it would fly. Meanwhile there was nothing for me to do but to stand around on the field and wait.

Hard on the nerves, because it gives you time to think, and you can't help calculating your chances. The speed of a man falling through the air is one hundred and twenty miles per hour; faster than that he won't fall, because of air resistance, but that is fast enough. It would give me three seconds for every five hundred feet. It would take keen timing not to pancake.

I didn't feel like talking, but a reporter came and questioned me: why jump parachutes? Someone had told him that the Army and Navy don't allow their men to do intentionals and that many civilian pilots don't even wear parachutes against emergencies, but prefer to take their chances sticking to their ships. What about that?

I told him what I had told myself so many times: that parachutes are required for certain maneuvers, and that therefore one might just as well know how to use them; that collision in the air is becoming the biggest and least calculable danger in aviation, and that after a collision only a 'chute will save you. I talked of fire in the air, structural failure, engine failure over rough country.

But then why make delayed jumps?

Again I could give him good enough reasons. How in war you might want to get down and out of shooting range in a hurry; how after a collision the wreckage sometimes falls almost as fast as the pilot, necessitating long delays in order to clear it. How pilots have bailed out because of an uncontrollable tailspin, and have then been chased by their ships almost down to the ground before they could rip. How in jumping from very fast ships you have so much speed that you might tear your canopy, or your harness, or your intestines, if you ripped right away; whereas if

[61]

you delay you actually slow down to mere falling speed. And how anyway, if you use life-saving equipment, you might as well be wholly familiar with it and learn to use it coolly.

The real reason, of course, he would not understand, nor would his readers; least of all would the farmer understand it into whose field, in case of mishap, the final mess would burst. The real reason was that a man likes to test his nerve and to get closer and closer and still a little closer to the edge of life.

They were now wheeling the ship out of the hangar. Time to get ready. Word had somehow spread and cars had come in from the highway. A small crowd was collecting, truck drivers, salesmen, store clerks off for lunch, hoping for a thrill.

The reporter wanted to know if I was married, and whether my mother knew about the jump.

Around and around in my head went a song I had once heard somewhere about "A Little Home in Flatbush." That was what I wanted just then, a little house and a complacent wife and never again any nerve testing. I had had enough of that.

The worst moment of a parachute jump comes when they dress you up and strap the 'chutes on you.

Moriturus: one who is about to die. That was my role as far as the crowd was concerned. They stood and gaped only because they thought they might see me die; yet I probably would not die; as a matter of fact I had a date in town for that afternoon. But just now my plans for more than a quarter hour ahead were somehow tentative and strangely uninteresting.

The field manager came to supervise the preparations, and must have seen me shiver in the cool wind. He took off his leather jacket and put it on me. He made me feel better. It kept the wind out, and it also showed that he did not expect to get it back all messed up with dead Langewiesche. The good old Swede.

The rigger and his assistant brought out the 'chutes. They had adjusted the harness. This time it gripped me tight around the legs and around the chest and over the shoulders. It almost hurt, but the feel was good; it pulled you together.

On top of that hung the heavy back pack. Then the chest pack for emergencies, buckled on in front. Heavy armor. It set you apart from the crowd, and marked you for a strange man off on a strange adventure.

It struck me that nobody wanted to talk to me. The men just stood around, watching. Beyond them, the ship was now noisily warming up its engine.

Again I could feel, by what little signs I could not tell, how some of the crowd was pulling for me but most of them against me. The field manager and the pilots and the flying students were for me, not because they liked me, not because they didn't think I was a fool, doing this without getting paid for it, but because they liked to think that parachutes always work. The rest were against me because they wanted a thrill; the reporter particularly was smelling blood.

The rigger alone was unexcited and workmanlike. He said, putting still another belt around me: "Now don't get mixed up, else you will be down before you know it."

Only the gray-haired little assistant—he who had been with the circuses for forty years—liked me. He reached down and rearranged the leg straps, to make sure I wouldn't be emasculated when the opening jerk hit. He spoke some German and he said: "*Mach's gut,*" calling me thou. He was pulling for me all right.

They put the flying helmet on me and fastened the chin strap, damping out the voices, shutting me off still further from the crowd. Then the goggles.

Only a few more minutes now. The pilot was climbing into the ship.

[63]

One girl was standing there among the men around me, the airport typist, or something like that. She alone now came through to me sharply, body and soul. For a moment I had an experience not given to many men in times of peace, thinking that she might be the last woman I should ever see. She was blond and good-looking. She was talking to a man while looking at me. But I could not make out whether she was pulling for me or against me.

The ship was ready. There was nothing more to discuss, nothing more to wait for, and I might as well go. It was clumsy walking with all that weight on me, and the rigger had to help me lower myself and my chest pack and my back pack into the front cockpit. Then he said, "O.K.," and stood back. We took off.

At three thousand five hundred feet, ready to take the jump, I stood outboard, on the root of the wing, on the trailing edge, facing the tail. It had been difficult to climb out with all that bulk strapped to me, and now I had to hold on with both hands to the fuselage, not to be blown off.

With the pilot I was almost face to face as he sat in his cockpit, looking forward, and I stood beside it, looking rearward. Close enough, but I felt alone. He was busy, scowling at his instruments, at the horizon, at the ground. He was trying to maneuver into a position that would land me—maybe—on the flying field. He didn't look at me, he didn't smile. There was no comradeship with him, merely the feeling of a job to be done. The job was to get away from each other smoothly. He hoped I would take a determined jump away from the ship, and that I would not pull prematurely and be blown into the tail and kill both of us. I hoped that he would give a well-timed kick on the rudder, the moment of jumping, to swing the tail out of my way. After that, we would worry each man for himself.

Around me was the empty world of the flier, the gray sky, the sad horizon. From the field, they were now probably watching breathlessly, but the field was small and far away; it was hard to distinguish among the farms. The town was small and far away, too. Word was spread and people were probably watching in the streets, but I was up here alone, shivering in the propeller wash, and all that didn't help me.

Below me was depth.

Looking down along my fluttering trouser legs I saw the tips of my shoes—good solid shoes for good solid sidewalks—stick out over the void. Far below them, creeping slowly, the farms, a highway, a factory chimney.

There was plenty of time to look down and to face it. Now, I would crash through the roof into a farm wife's soup; now, I would be impaled on a telegraph pole; now, a little wood, much more inviting—the tree tops looked soft and bouncy.

Nervously, I went over the top. I wanted to jump. Not much fear was left. My nerves themselves at last remembered again the experience of the first jump; the big fall that had not ended in a catastrophic hit, but in that wide, joyous rip across my chest; the opening shock that had jerked me all over heaven; and, after that, the comfortable sensation as I floated down. Some animal fear of falling might indeed spring up again the moment of actually stepping off, but the thing to do against that was to concentrate on the first few moments of falling, to control myself, and not to pull the ripcord.

The pilot throttled back the engine and went into a glide. He nodded.

It was up to me.

I let go with my hands. Immediately the air stream bowled me over. A cold shock; my right hand gripped frantically all over my left shoulder and chest for the ripcord and couldn't grab it.

[65]

Balance was already gone, there was no stopping. A quick look, and I found it. Then I kicked myself off, away from the ship.

Down I went in a violent, breathless, silent tumble. The bottom dropped out from under me, from under my brains, my intestines. I couldn't see, I couldn't hear. I only felt I was going to smash.

Now was the time to hold it.

My hand was on the ring, but I must stand this until I could stand it absolutely no longer.

I must hold it still a little longer.

My head cleared, my breath came again, and I saw the ground. It was only a brief glimpse, but it was enough. I had won over the first confusion. I had not ripped, and now the ground was still far away, and there was still plenty of time.

I was falling face downward.

The ground was steady. It was not rushing up to meet me, as water rushes up when you dive off a spring board. It didn't move at all. At this rate, I could keep falling forever.

The fall rolled me over on my side, and then on my back. Between my feet, I could now see the horizon, and against the horizon, the ship. It was flying away from me, and doing a curve. Watching it, watching the familiar rhythm of an airplane in flight, gave me back my sense of timing. I got a good look at it, marveling all the while that there was so much time, jumping down from the sky. I could see how I was losing height fast; for although the ship's nose was down and it was gliding, it seemed to float upwards rapidly.

A new twist, and I lost sight of it.

I was picking up more speed every instant, and I could feel it in my innards. It was the law of gravitation, at work on a falling body, and felt from the inside out. One moment it felt as if I had been merely loafing around. A moment later I seemed to be dropping away like a stone.

Yet, there was still no hurry. I could see the horizon and by it could tell that I was still 'way up.

It may have been three or four seconds after jumping, but it felt more like six or seven, when I first became conscious of the thickness of the air. There was a new sensation. I was no longer dropping through a void.

A bottom was back under things, a soft but firm bottom of air rushing up against me from underneath. I could feel my back lying on it, the calves of my legs, and my arm and hand. It took all the fright out of falling. It was the same thing that holds you up in flying, and that fliers get a feeling for and learn to trust: air plus motion.

The tumbling began again. My head was heavier than the rest of me, and sank faster. I felt myself sliding off my air mattress backwards, headfirst. A glimpse of my own legs, flailing against the clouds. Overhead, which was now below, a flash of green ground. Then the legs fell over in a nasty backwards somersault. It didn't feel safe at all. I almost let her rip.

Somehow I got stabilized again, falling face downward, lying flat on the air stream, lying comfortably, with face, chest, belly, legs, arm, fingers, on a solid transparent nothing; and looking down through it, too. I fell steadily now, not speeding up any more. I had reached terminal velocity, one hundred and twenty miles per hour or thereabouts, and it felt fine. I had worried about it, and about the sharp timing that would be required. But now it wasn't like falling at all, more like flying, and I was quite relaxed. The ground was coming up, but only slowly. I saw a highway, white through the green grass land. I saw the farm I was falling into getting steadily bigger, as if being pulled up by a magnifying lens.

This was comfortable. It took three seconds perhaps, but it seemed longer.

Then the air stream gave me a new twist. I began to roll over sideways, and my head sank away again. I began to wonder if I hadn't better pull now, while the 'chute could still string out away from my body. I might be all the way down before I would be again in a favorable position. I was still wondering when the farm suddenly took a lunge, blew up, and exploded in my face.

I was THERE.

I managed to pull the ripcord quite slowly, deliberately, with no particular force. So much had the feel of the air stream taken the catastrophe out of falling. I could feel the latch pins snap open; the ripcord, a little farther out, was getting stuck; for safety's sake I gave it another easy pull and got it all the way out.

There was again that ugly split second when you have a piece of slack wire rope in your hand. You can do no more with it, and nothing happens.

Then the big jerk—vicious, quite unelastic. I might as well have lassoed a locomotive. It hurt plenty, but it was all over in a moment. I hung.

Of all the sensations of air-faring, that is the most dreamlike—floating under a parachute. It begins with a wave of triumphal emotion which is standard accompaniment of everyone's first parachute jump and is unlike any other experience—there is in it the sudden deliverance from danger, also release from perhaps the most concentrated bit of waiting there is, and also exultation of being high up in the air, flying for once in silence, for once almost without a machine.

I looked up at my 'chute—the simplest of all aircraft. It quivered, high above me, the merest handkerchief in size; it seemed incredible that so small a bit of silk should have so much holding power. In the stillness it gave out a thin sound, like a peanut whistle. That was the air, escaping through its center vent hole. It was a warning, though I didn't understand it: an indication of the speed with which I was actually coming down.

For the time being, I was well afloat with my magic carpet. The harness was holding up my weight so evenly that I was hardly conscious of it. It was like flying in dreams, flying simply because you are light. My feet were limp under me, hanging into a cornfield. The view was the usual one from an airplane, the green plain, the distant horizon. But there was no wind; when I moved my hand, the air felt thin.

I heard excited shouts of children from somewhere. I found I was very low; I hadn't pulled any too soon. There was no time to enjoy the floating down. I was drifting onto a telephone line— or was it high tension? I grabbed two of the shrouds above me and pulled on them, sideslipping the 'chute into an open field. It was dark bare earth, with yesterday's rains still on it in pools. The slip made me swing viciously, pendulum fashion. I was worried about the landing, but there was no time left to steady myself. I was falling through fast. I went limp, and hit.

This time I hit very lightly; it must have been because of the cool, heavy air. I sat down, but only because I was limp. I could have taken it standing. The canopy was still open and tugged in the wind. I pulled on one shroud until it collapsed. I got up and looked around for someone to come and greet me and help me. I had landed far from the flying field. I was alone except for some cows. The ship was gone from the sky.

I unbuckled the harness and rolled up the silk. Still nobody was in sight, and I loaded my seventy pounds of parachute on my shoulders and started walking, ankle deep in black soft soil.

THE FRIGATE PELICAN
by Marianne Moore

Rapidly cruising or lying on the air there is a bird
   that realizes Rasselas's friend's project
   of wings uniting levity with strength. This
     hell-diver, frigate-bird, hurricane-
bird; unless swift is the proper word
   for him, the storm omen when
   he flies close to the waves, should be seen
     fishing, although oftener
     he appears to prefer

to take, on the wing, from industrious cruder-winged species
   the fish they have caught, and is seldom successless.
   A marvel of grace, no matter how fast his
     victim may fly or how often may
turn, the dishonest pelican's ease
   in pursuit, bears him away
   with the fish that the badgered bird drops.
     A kind of superlative
     swallow, that likes to live

on food caught while flying, he is not a pelican. The toe
   with slight web, air-boned body, and very long wings
   with the spread of a swan's—duplicating a
     bow-string as he floats overhead—feel

the changing V-shaped scissor swallow-
    tail direct the rigid keel.
  And steering beak to windward always,
      the fleetest foremost fairy
      among birds, outflies the

aeroplane which cannot flap its wings nor alter any quill-
    tip. For him, the feeling in a hand, in fins, is
    in his unbent downbent crafty oar. With him
      other pelicans aimlessly soar
as he does; separating, until
    not flapping they rise once more,
  closing in without looking and move
      outward again to the top
      of the circle and stop

and blow back. The lugubrious ragged immense minuet
   descending to leeward, ascending to windward
   again without flapping, in what seems to be
    a way of resting, are now nearer,
but as seemingly bodiless yet
    as they were. Theirs are sombre
  quills for so wide and light-boned a bird
      as the frigate pelican
      of the Caribbean.

MALLARD
by Rex Warner

Squawking they rise from reeds into the sun,
climbing like furies, running on blood and bone,
with wings like garden shears clipping the misty air,
four mallard, hard winged, with necks like rods
fly in perfect formation over the marsh.

Keeping their distance, gyring, not letting slip the air,
but leaping into it straight like hounds or divers,
they stretch out into the wind and sound their horns again.

Suddenly siding to a bank of air unbidden
by hand signal or morse message of command
down sky they plane, sliding like corks on a current,
designed so deftly that all air is advantage,

till with few flaps, orderly as they left earth,
alighting amid curlew they pad on mud.

The Nuptial Flight of the Queen Bee
by Maurice Maeterlinck

Around the virgin queen, and dwelling with her in the hive, are hundreds of exuberant males, forever drunk on honey; the sole reason for their existence being one act of love. But, notwithstanding the incessant contact of two desires that elsewhere invariably triumph over every obstacle, the union never takes place in the hive, nor has it been possible to bring about the impregnation of a captive queen. While she lives in their midst the lovers about her know not what she is. They seek her in space, in the remote depths of the horizon, never suspecting that they have but this moment quitted her, have shared the same comb with her, have brushed against her, perhaps, in the eagerness of their departure. One might almost believe that those wonderful eyes of theirs, that cover their head as though with a glittering helmet, do not recognize or desire her save when she soars in the blue. Each day, from noon till three, when the sun shines resplendent, this plumed hoard sallies forth in search of the bride, who is indeed more royal, more difficult of conquest, than the most inaccessible princess of fairy legend; for twenty or thirty tribes will hasten from all the neighboring cities, her court thus consisting of more than ten thousand suitors; and from these ten thousand one alone will be chosen for the unique kiss of an instant that shall wed him to death no less than to happiness; while the others will fly helplessly round the intertwined pair, and soon will perish without ever again beholding this prodigious and fatal apparition.

Nature is always magnificent when dealing with the privileges and prerogatives of love. She becomes miserly only when doling out the organs and instruments of labor. She is especially severe on what men have termed virtue, whereas she strews the path of the most uninteresting lovers with innumerable jewels and favors. "Unite and multiply; there is no other law, or aim, than love," would seem to be her constant cry on all sides, while she mutters to herself, perhaps: "and exist afterwards if you can; that is no concern of mine." Do or desire what else we may, we find, everywhere on our road, this morality that differs so much from our own.

Very few, I imagine, have profaned the secret of the queen-bee's wedding, which comes to pass in the infinite, radiant circles of a beautiful sky. But we are able to witness the hesitating departure of the bride-elect and the murderous return of the bride.

However great her impatience, she will yet choose her day and her hour, and linger in the shadow of the portal till a marvellous morning fling open wide the nuptial spaces in the depths of the great azure vault. She loves the moment when drops of dew still moisten the leaves and the flowers, when the last fragrance of dying dawn still wrestles with burning day, like a maiden caught in the arms of a heavy warrior; when through the silence of approaching noon is heard, once and again, a transparent cry that has lingered from sunrise.

Then she appears on the threshold—in the midst of indifferent foragers, if she have left sisters in the hive; or surrounded by a delirious throng of workers, should it be impossible to fill her place.

She starts her flight backwards; returns twice or thrice to the alighting-board; and then, having definitely fixed in her mind the exact situation and aspect of the kingdom she has never yet seen from without, she departs like an arrow to the zenith of the blue. She soars to a height, a luminous zone, that other bees attain at no period of their life. Far away, caressing their idleness in the midst of the flowers, the males have beheld the apparition, have breathed the magnetic perfume that spreads from group to group till every apiary near is instinct with it. Immediately crowds collect, and follow her into the sea of gladness, whose limpid boundaries ever recede. She, drunk with her wings, obeying the magnificent law of the race that chooses her lover, and enacts that the strongest alone shall attain her in the solitude of the ether, she rises still; and for the first time in her life, the blue morning air rushes into her stigmata, singing its song, like the blood of heaven, in the myriad tubes of the tracheal sacs, nourished on space, that fill the centre of her body. She rises still. A region must be found unhaunted by birds, that else might profane the mystery. She rises still; and already the ill-assorted troop below are dwindling and falling asunder. The feeble, infirm, the aged, unwelcome, ill-fed, who have flown from inactive or impoverished cities, these renounce the pursuit and disappear in the void. Only a small, indefatigable cluster remain, suspended in infinite opal. She summons her wings for one final effort; and now the chosen of incomprehensible forces has reached her, has seized her, and bounding aloft with united impetus, the ascending spiral of their intertwined flight whirls for one second in the hostile madness of love.

Most creatures have a vague belief that a very precarious hazard, a kind of transparent membrane, divides death from love; and that the profound idea of nature demands that the giver of life should die at the moment of giving. Here this idea, whose memory lingers still over the kisses of man, is realized in its primal simplicity. No sooner has the union been accomplished than the male's abdomen opens, the organ detaches itself, dragging with it the mass of the entrails; the wings relax, and, as though struck by lightning, the emptied body turns and turns on itself and sinks down into the abyss.

Prodigious nuptials these, the most fairylike that can be conceived, azure and tragic, raised high above life by the impetus of desire; imperishable and terrible, unique and bewildering, solitary and infinite. An admirable ecstasy, wherein death supervening in all that our sphere has of most limpid and loveliest, in virginal, limitless space, stamps the instant of happiness in the sublime transparence of the great sky; purifying in that immaculate light the something of wretchedness that always hovers around love, rendering the kiss one that can never be forgotten; and, content this time with moderate tithe, proceeding herself, with hands that are almost maternal, to introduce and unite, in one body, for a long and inseparable future, two fragile lives.

The Caged Eagle's Death Dream
(from *Cawdor*)

by Robinson Jeffers

At the one shot
The great bird leaped at the roof of the cage
In silence and struck the wood; it fell, then suddenly
Looked small and soft, muffled in its folded wings.

The nerves of men after they die dream dimly
And dwindle into their peace; they are not very passionate,
And what they had was mostly spent while they lived.
They are sieves for leaking desire; they have many pleasures
And conversations; their dreams too are like that.
The unsocial birds are a greater race;
Cold-eyed, and their blood burns. What leaped up to death,
The extension of one storm-dark wing filling its world,
Was more than the soft garment that fell. Something had flown
    away. Oh cage-hoarded desire,
Like the blade of a breaking wave reaped by the wind, or flame
    rising from fire, or cloud-coiled lightning
Suddenly unfurled in the cave of heaven: I that am stationed, and
    cold at heart, incapable of burning,
My blood like standing sea-water lapped in a stone pool, my
    desire to the rock, how can I speak of you?
Mine will go down to the deep rock.

                      This rose,

Possessing the air over its emptied prison,
The eager powers at its shoulders waving shadowless
Unwound the ever-widened spirals of flight
As a star light, it spins the night-stabbing threads
From its own strength and substance: so the aquiline desire
Burned itself into meteor freedom and spired
Higher still, and saw the mountain-dividing
Canyon of its captivity (that was to Cawdor
Almost his world) like an old crack in a wall,
Violet-shadowed and gold-lighted; the little stain
Spilt on the floor of the crack was the strong forest;
The grain of sand was the Rock. A speck, and atomic
Center of power clouded in its own smoke
Ran and cried in the crack; it was Cawdor; the other
Points of humanity had neither weight nor shining
To prick the eyes of even an eagle's passion.

This burned and soared. The shining ocean below lay on the
    shore
Like the great shield of the moon come down, rolling bright rim
    to rim with the earth. Against it the multiform
And many-canyoned coast-range hills were gathered into one
    carven mountain, one modulated
Eagle's cry made stone, stopping the strength of the sea. The
    beaked and winged effluence
Felt the air foam under its throat and saw
The mountain sun-cup Tassajara, where fawns
Dance in the steam of the hot fountains at dawn,
Smoothed out, and the high strained ridges beyond Cachagua,
Where the rivers are born and the last condor is dead,
Flatten, and a hundred miles toward morning the Sierras

Dawn with their peaks of snow, and dwindle and smooth down
On the globed earth.

It saw from the height and desert space of
    unbreathable air
Where meteors make green fire and die, the ocean dropping
    westward to the girdle of the pearls of dawn
And the hinder edge of the night sliding toward Asia; it saw
    far under eastward the April-delighted
Continent; and time relaxing about it now, abstracted from
    being, it saw the eagles destroyed,
Mean generations of gulls and crows taking their world: turn
    for turn in the air, as on earth
The white faces drove out the brown. It saw the white decayed
    and the brown from Asia returning;
It saw men learn to outfly the hawk's brood and forget it again;
    it saw men cover the earth and again
Devour each other and hide in caverns, be scarce as wolves. It
    neither wondered nor cared, and it saw
Growth and decay alternate forever, and the tides returning.

It saw, according to the sight of its kind, the archetype
Body of life a beaked carnivorous desire
Self-upheld on storm-broad wings: but the eyes
Were spouts of blood; the eyes were gashed out; dark blood
Ran from the ruinous eye-pits to the hook of the beak
And rained on the waste spaces of empty heaven.
Yet the great Life continued; yet the great Life
Was beautiful, and she drank her defeat, and devoured
Her famine for food.
                    There the eagle's phantom perceived
Its prison and its wound were not its peculiar wretchedness,

All that lives was maimed and bleeding, caged or in blindness,
Lopped at the ends with death and conception, and shrewd
Cautery of pain on the stumps to stifle the blood, but not
Refrains for all that; life was more than its functions
And accidents, more important than its pains and pleasures,
A torch to burn in with pride, a necessary
Ecstasy in the run of the cold substance,
And scape-goat of the greater world. (But as for me,
I have heard the summer dust crying to be born
As much as ever flesh cried to be quiet.)
Pouring itself on fulfilment the eagle's passion
Left life behind and flew at the sun, its father.
The great unreal talons took peace for prey
Exultantly, their death beyond death; stooped upward, and
    struck
Peace like a white fawn in a dell of fire.

PART IV

Apprentice Stages

Sul Volo degli Uccelli

by Leonardo da Vinci

(*Translated by Edward MacCurdy*)

The great bird will take its first flight upon the back of the great swan, filling the whole world with amazement and filling all records with its fame; and it will bring eternal glory to the nest where it was born.

If water strikes the tail of the fish which is in the axis above the centre of its accidental gravity there is no doubt that this fish will bend round this centre; but its tail will bend more in the current of the water than its trunk will, for this being firmer offers more resistance in its contrary movement.

The impetus which was circular in its commencement may follow out in itself the same circular movement upon its axis as that of the millstone or the revolving wheel, and may follow it circular or straight, as the wheel of the cart revolving naturally outside of its axis or as the reflex movement made in a slanting line by the spherical bodies. Similarly, the flight of birds, even though the beginning of the bird's impulse may be caused by direct movement, may continue in circular movement for as great a distance as this impetus endures.

The level movement of birds when they fly may swiftly be changed either to a slanting or vertical movement towards the sky or towards the earth. The movement towards the sky occurs when the helms of the wings and also the tail are turned towards the earth.

When a bird is descending it keeps a straighter course and has less risk of being overturned if it has its wings bent beneath it than if it keeps them straight.

When a bird's centre of gravity is below its wings it has so much the less risk of being turned upside down, as is seen above.

Make a small one, to go over the water, and try it in the wind without much depth of water over some part of the Arno, with the wind natural, and then as you please, and turn the sail and the helm.

See tomorrow to all these matters, and the copies, and then efface the originals and leave them at Florence, so that if you lose those that you take with you the invention will not be lost. . . .

There is as much power of movement in the water or the air against an object as there is in this object against the air or the water.

The centre of gravity of the fish lying level in the water or of the bird lying level in the air is situated midway between the extremities which offer equal resistance.

Write of swimming under water and you will have the flight of the bird through the air. There is a suitable place there where the mills discharge into the Arno, by the falls of Ponte Rubaconte.

There are two different ways in which a bird can turn in any direction while continually beating its wings. The first of these is when at the same time it moves one wing more rapidly downwards than the other with an equal degree of force, the movement approximating towards the tail; the second is when in the same space of time the movement of one wing is longer than that of the other. Also in striking with the wings downwards slantwise, if they become bent or moved one lower down and the other farther back, the part which drives the wing lower down will be higher in the first case, and the opposite part of the wings which has the longer movement backward will go farther forward through this first; consequently for this reason the movement of the bird will form a curve round that part of it which is highest.

These then are all the movements made by the bird without beating its wings, and they are each and all subject to a single rule, for all these movements rise upon the wind, for they expose themselves to it slantwise receiving it under their wings after the manner of a wedge.

A bird is an instrument working according to mathematical law, which instrument it is within the capacity of man to reproduce with all its movements, but not with a corresponding degree of strength, though it is deficient only in the power of maintaining equilibrium. We may therefore say that such an instrument constructed by man is lacking in nothing except the life of the bird, and this life must needs be supplied by that of man.

The life which resides in the bird's members will without doubt better conform to their needs than will that of man which is separated from them, and especially in the almost imperceptible movements which preserve equilibrium. But since we see that the bird is equipped for many obvious varieties of movements, we are able from this experience to declare that the most rudimentary of these movements will be capable of being comprehended by man's understanding; and that he will to a great extent be able to provide against the destruction of that instrument of which he has himself become the living principle and the propeller.

If a man have a tent made of linen of which the apertures have all been stopped up, and it be twelve braccia across and twelve in depth, he will be able to throw himself down from any great height without sustaining any injury.

Observe how the beating of its wings against the air suffices to bear up the weight of the eagle in the highly rarefied air which borders on the fiery element! Observe also how the air moving over the sea, beaten back by the bellying sails, causes the heavily laden ship to glide onwards!

By adducing and expounding the reasons of these things you may be able to realize that man when he has great wings attached to him, by exerting his strength against the resistance of the air and conquering it, is enabled to subdue it and to raise himself upon it.

THE EMPIRE OF THE AIR
by L. P. Mouillard

If there be a domineering, tyrant thought, it is the conception that the problem of flight may be solved by man. When once this idea has invaded the brain it possesses it exclusively. It becomes a haunting thought, a walking nightmare impossible to shake. And if we consider the pitying contempt in which such a line of research is held, we may conceive the unhappy lot of the poor investigator whose soul is thus possessed. Many of them, either through pride or through timidity, have withdrawn themselves from human intercourse, and thus have found themselves paralyzed attempting to carry on their researches in secret.

In studying the maneuvers of birds, close proximity is greatly to be desired. . . . In Cairo it is easy to touch the Kite in full flight by going about it skillfully, but the most stirring, exciting sight (the word is not too strong) is to stand in the Vulture roost on the Mokatan ridge near Cairo and to watch the *Gyps fulvus* pass within five yards in full flight. How useless to try to describe this spectacle! When these enormous birds rush past, an astonishing rustling may be heard. The great primary feathers vibrate like tongues of steel, flexing upward to a quarter circle under the fifteen pounds of bird they bear. . . . But a Condor whose pectoral muscles could produce the lightning beats of a warbler's wings must indeed have pinions of metal, and their roaring would be as thunder.

I was convinced *a priori* that an expert soarer could, in a fresh breeze, rise directly into the air and advance against the wind. I felt sure that the feat was feasible. I waited for years before witnessing it. At last one day in Africa two eagles in love afforded me the spectacle. One of them launched from the top of the ash tree that served as a perch, descended against the wind six to ten feet, was raised by a gust of wind, and thus continued to rise, slowly, steadily, a hundred yards into the air, while he also advanced some fifty yards against the wind without a single beat or impulse of his mighty wings. Such convincing demonstrations are not to be seen every day. They must be persistently awaited. The observer must burn with the sacred fire. He must be drawn to the study of flying creatures by that indefinable enthusiasm which causes his heart to hammer when he sees certain evolutions.

To rightly explain the flight of birds, however, we must consider them as highly organized machines, sustained by the reactions produced by muscular effort; not as a balloon floating the air, but as a stone glancing along water or as a skater gliding over thin ice. All that apparatus described for distending the Gannet, all those porous bones of the Pelican and the Albatross, serve flight in no degree. . . . The proportion of the Albatross—twenty to one—should be borne in mind in the design of aeroplanes with adjustable surfaces. But the Teal and the Duck are the representatives of rapidity of flight. They flap to excess, supplied as they are with carbon by the heavy layer of oily fat which covers their pectoral muscles, and this is the type to imitate for aviation with motors. Mechanical science will eventually furnish quite a number of different solutions, such as flapping wings, propelling screws, rocket propulsion. . . . But ascension itself need be merely the result of the skillful use of the power of the wind, and no other force is required.

Pelicans, in their travel, arrange themselves as a wedge. They move with a curious sluggishness, and with the regularity of iron rolling-mill machines. These enormous palmipedes sometimes afford a most engrossing spectacle. I remember one day upon the Nile to have seen a flock of them come sailing out of the sky, dropping from a height where first they seemed as Swallows, alighting within two hundred yards of my boat on one of those gelatinous islands of mud peculiar to that river. For an hour I followed all their evolutions through a telescope. It was astonishing how beautiful these great birds were as they wheeled among the clouds. From afar off one could hear the hissing of their wings as they cut the air, their hoarse cries, and even the slap of their great feet as they struck the liquid mud.

The act of alighting is the terror of all winged creatures and happy are those which descend upon the water. The Swan comes down to her liquid bed, and striking is the spectacle as she ploughs deep furrows with her palmed feet, throwing up jets of water and foam.

But finally let us admit that the problem has been solved, and let us speculate upon the effects on society. Let us begin with property. Property will be riven with an enormous gap. With the patent insufficiency of enclosure, with intrusion into the privacy of homes—hedges and walls will no longer be of service. The enclosure under the roof will be incomplete. And all this will constitute a curtailment of the privileges of possession, a diminished efficiency of barriers.

What of the collectors of customs and the police in the presence of this new mode of locomotion? What will these officers do when they must watch the air, that immense pathway some four or five miles high? During the day it may be possible to fancy some partly satisfactory surveillance; with a large force, good telescopes, fast cruisers of the air, we might perhaps exercise some control; but at night what is to be done? How can we bar the empire of the air? How can we so much as watch it when opaque fog annihilates the effect of electric reflectors?

With the suppression of the custom-house what will become of revenues and the balancing of the budget? These disturbances to property, to customs, to the police, are mere bagatelles when compared to the revolution that will result in political matters. All will have to be done over again; the fortifications, the maneuvers, the defenses of the frontiers, strategy, all is reduced to nothing. It will even cause, in a very short time, the suppression of nationalities; and races will be rapidly commingled or destroyed, for there will no longer be efficient barriers, not even that movable barrier which we call an army. No more frontiers! No more insular seclusion! No more fortifications! Will society perish?

As to the procedure that society will adopt to conform to this new mode of existence, I have not the least idea, yet it may be affirmed that society will emerge victorious from the struggle. After the cataclysm caused by injured interests, a period of restored equilibrium will follow; and in the end, at the expense of a time of distress, humanity will enter into possession of the empire of the air.

1881

THE PIONEERS
by Selden Rodman

Thousands are building; in byways and backways, unpressed by
    profit, then bought by it,

The cold plow turns the land; the duplex telegraph says Yes and
    No; the first

Web press and linotype machine convert the forests into what?

The burning plain is crossed by the refrigerator car; the voice
    from a machine

Sings Mary Had a Little Lamb; the figure of a man upon a
    screen

Moves silently, flickering; the ears at the receiver hear;

And everywhere the frequencies of hope ask breathlessly whether
    the brain

Has established communication between men, has conquered the
    ancient fear.

Humboldt on Chimborazo studied the condor; Darwin com-
    pared wing motion to a sculling oar;

Marey computed ratios of weight-to-wingspread; Pettigrew
    ascribed to gravity, drift;

Means said: "It will be done because the air is solid if you hit
    it hard enough . . ."

When the biologists and artists got together the smoke of in-
    dustry began to lift.

They studied form. Langley deduced the horsepower by measuring a pterodactyl's bone.

Tachometers took shape when sailors checked the tags on birds that crossed the ocean.

They recognized the economy of nature in the buzzard's yacht-like sails

No less than in the engine-crowded hummingbird. They studied motion.

Lilienthal with his brother in North Germany hears the fable of the willow-wren

Riding the stork's back: at midnight in the cemetery they trap butterflies;

Notice, with the wind behind them, how storks hop *toward* them in fright;

Their father, preparing to emigrate to mechanical America, dies.

On the Potsdam drill-ground they experiment nightly to avoid laughter.

When Otto is drafted for the war with the French, he returns shouting: "Now, wings!"

In the attic their fingers bleed at the tips from quills and palisander sticks;

At Spandau Road they build kites in the form of birds controlled by strings.

Maxim, between artillery work, studies wind-currents over rolling land.

Pilcher in the Royal Navy, hearing of Lilienthal, forgets war.

The American builder of bridges and stockyards, at the age of seventy-two

Retires—to test the conditions of equilibrium on the dunes of the South Shore.

And across Lake Michigan in Dayton, the vibrations of that
    hope awake
Such joy as the rescuer feels when he signals he can reach the
    ship;
Abandoning Inherent Stability, the arbitrary creature of the gale,
They look for the principle of operator's touch upon body and
    arched wingtip,
Deferring principles of power: what furnaces Force might mount
On Atlas-shoulders challenging heaven but subservient to earth,
    is deferred;
Oblivious to the triumph of the wind-bag whose motor-driven
    day has come,
Their faith in the body is unshaken. They return to the study
    of the bird.

Knowing no bird is lighter than the air, that insect, bat or bird
    falling
Converts that weight, or gravity, or what you will, in such a way
That like the albatross, all motionless but for the turning
Of eye on prey, the Australian crane so ponderous of pinion,
Or frigate bird: the wind is made to work, the air uphold
Expanding tail; stretched neck must form the proper planes,
Shifting the center but controlled at will . . . Their will
Fortified by these facts, calls the balloon "the great misleader"
Refusing to be satisfied with less than natural skill;
Experience, less wholly free than birds', disdains.

Spiraling through their minds to consciousness, the dream has
    not yet cast
The shadow of its wings upon their world. They only see,
Childlike, the dimensions of a bright universe where fear
And fire from the clouds are dragons of the unreal night.

"We will cross chasms," they say, "accompanied only by the
    wind,
Earth's jarring combat left below, we who believe in buoyancy
Will train the eye by gradual ascent, free, motionless, suspended
    there
To look upon earth's perilous landscape unconcernedly . . ."

But ages mix. Their toy demands the weight of industry upon
    its back.
Will Otto find the bridge-truss that Chanute has brought enough
To lift four cylinders? Is Pilcher in "The Hawk" prepared
To give Lord Braye an exhibition in bad weather? Is the gruff
Smithsonian professor ready to go beyond
The ballistics of bluejays, the wingspread of gnat and chick?
Has Ader's political party the right amount of "pull"?
Can all the sandpaper in the world make Maxim's propellers
    click?

They asked no monuments. They were rivals; but for fun
Who asked fearlessly before their time for wings to raise them.
Let the patent-offices take care of their return. The response to
    an open "gun"
Or a three-point landing should be enough to praise them.

THE STRUCTURE OF THE PLANE
by Muriel Rukeyser

Kitty Hawk is a Caesar among monuments;
    the stiff bland soldiers predestined to their death
    the bombs piled neatly like children's marbles piled
    sperm to breed corpses eugenically by youth
    out of seductive death.
                    The hill outdoes our towers
    we might treasure a thistle grown from a cannon-mouth
    they have not permitted rust and scum and blossoms
    to dirty the steel,
                however we have the plane
the hill, flower among monuments.

"To work intelligently" (Orville and Wilbur Wright)
"one needs to know the effects of variations
incorporated in the surfaces. . . . The pressures on squares
are different from those on rectangles, circles, triangles, or el-
    lipses. . . .
The shape of the edge also makes a difference."

The plane is wheeled out of the hangar. The sleeves shake
fixing the wind, the four o'clock blue sky
blinks in the goggles swinging over his wrist.
The plane rests, the mechanic in cream-colored overalls
encourages the engine into idling speed.

The instructor looks at his class
and begins the demonstration.

"We finally became discouraged, and returned to kite-flying.
But as we grew older we had to give up this sport,
it was unbecoming to boys of our ages."

On the first stroke of the piston the intake valve opens,
the piston moves slowly from the head of the cylinder,
drawing in its mixture of gas and air. On the second stroke
the piston returns, the valve closes. The mixture is compressed.
A spark occurs, igniting America, opening India,
finding the Northwest Passage, Cipango spice,
causing the mixture to burn, expanding the gases
which push the piston away on the power stroke.
The final exhaust stroke serves to release the gases,
allowing the piston to scavenge the cylinder.
    We burn space, we sever galaxies,
      solar systems whirl about Shelley's head,
      we give ourselves ease, gentlemen, art and these explosions
      and Peter Ronsard finger-deep in roses:
gentlemen, remember these incandescent points,
remember to check, remember to drain the oil,
remember Plato O remember me
    the college pathways rise
    the president's voice intoning sonnets
    the impress of hoofmarks on the bridle path
    the shining girls the lost virginities
    the plane over a skeletal water-tower
    our youth dissolving O remember
    romantically dissolving remember me.

Blue smoke from the exhaust signifies too much oil.
Save yourselves from excesses, dirt, and tailspins.
These are the axioms: stability, control,
and equilibrium: in a yaw, in a roll, or pitch.
Here, gentlemen, are the wings, of fabric doped and painted
here is the rudder
here the propeller spins
BE hammers in the brain
FLY and the footbeat of that drum
may not be contradicted
must be mine
must be made ours, say the brothers Wright together
    although the general public had been invited
    few dared a cold December
    in order to see another plane not fly.

The helmet is strapped tight, orders are shouted
the elbows of steel move in oil
air is forced under the ship, the pilot's hand
is safe on the stick, the young student sits
with the wind mottling his eyelashes, rigidly.
Centuries fall behind his brain, the motor
pushes in a four-beat rhythm, his blood moves,
he dares look at the levels mounting in clouds
the dropping fields of the sky the diminishment of earth;
    now he thinks I am the child crying Mother
    this rim is the threshold into the hall's night
    or the windowsill livened with narcissus.
    The white edge of the bath a moment before
    slipping into watery ease, the windowsill
    eager for the jump into the street
    the hard stone under my back, the earth

with its eyes and hands its eyes and hands
its eyes
                fixed eyes on the diminishing
take me back the bath had fronds of steam
escaping the hands held my head
my eyes slipped in oil looking along your beauty
earth is painful the distance hurts
mother the night, the distance, dear
he is standing with one look of hate upon him
screams at the pilot you bastard, you bastard, jumps
trailing a long scream above him, the plane yaws down,
the motor pulls heavily, the ground is dark November,
his parachute opens a bright plume surrendering downward,
the plane heads up again, no good in following,
continues unfascinated by night or land or death.

PALM ISLAND PLANE FACTORY
by Francis Chichester

The *Makambo* returned from Sydney; she brought materials for me, and I began rebuilding the wings. Often, lying awake at night, I feared I had undertaken more than I could perform. And the first thing I read on studying the blue-print sent was that each bay of the wing must be trammelled to 15/100 inch. "Wing" I knew, and "bay" I knew, but:

"Roly, what is a trammel?" I asked.

"Trammel!" said he. "Isn't that what a bishop carries when preaching in a cathedral?"

"It seems to me that fooling round with this blue-print will get us into an unholy mess. I think we had better throw it away, remember how the broken wing comes to pieces, and rebuild it just the same. When in doubt, ask mother-wit."

"That's just what I think, too," said Roly.

But it occurred to me that it might be easier said than done.

"Roly," I said, "there appear to be thirty riblets in this wing, and ten ribs, of which seven have one shape, and the others each a different shape."

"That's what it looks like to me," said Roly.

"So that, if we first strip off the ten old ribs—then build on ten new ribs—provided, of course, that they are of correct shape, in correct place, and fastened to the spars exactly as the old ribs were fastened—that's all there is to it. Apart, that is to say, from

[99]

riblets, fillets, slots, leading-edges, trailing-edges and that sort of thing."

"Exactly what I think," said Roly.

Each rib was made of twenty-one pieces of spruce no thicker than thick cardboard; yet every piece must be in place, glued there and tacked, and the rib fit tightly on to the spars. However, we plugged away, and slowly the job seemed to yield us its secrets. Until, at the end of a week's work, we knew something about aeroplane construction. We could fit trailing-edges; plug and glue old screw-holes; cut, glue and tack old pieces of rib together; and clean, screw, measure, saw, shave and shape like a pair of factory robots. A curious thing was to find every inter-spar metal strut inside the wing to be full of sea-water, though five weeks had already elapsed since the plane was wrecked. I said to Roly: "We must drill holes in the metal struts to let out that water."

"That's just what I think," he said.

Next morning I said to him: "You know I think we ought to drill through the woodwork to let that water out."

"Do you know," said Roly, "after you left yesterday I was thinking just the same thing."

Next morning I said: "Roly, I think after all that we should drill the metal struts themselves to let that water out."

"Well, now," said he, "how curious! Because that's just what occurred to me after you had gone yesterday."

We finished the woodwork of the first wing. It looked pretty good to me. We prepared for its cover by painting it, in the first place, with water-proof lionoil. Every corner, stick and cranny had to be well done. Secondly, it needed a coat of dope-resisting paint to prevent the cover from sticking to each rib. The trouble was to find this paint. We had forty gallons altogether, and went round and round in solemn procession, Roly and I, inspecting every label. But however hard we looked, none of them would read "Dope-resisting Paint." Yet it was on the invoice, so must be there. The only tin not otherwise accounted for was one labelled "Thinners."

"I suppose that must be it," said I.

"I suppose so, too," said Roly; so we slapped on a coat of "thinners" before laying a piece of the light-brown linen fabric, fourteen feet by ten feet, on the frame for a cover. The question was, should the cover be sewn on tight or loose? Roly and I disagreed. I said the dope would shrink it tight, so that, if sewn on tight at the start, it would split in half when doped. "Sew it on loose," said I. "No, sew it on tight," said Roly. By nightfall, we still had not agreed, so left it draped over the wing skeleton. Next morning, I said: "You know, Roly, I believe you are right and it ought to be sewn on tight."

"That's a funny thing," he said, "because I was just thinking you were right and that it ought to be sewn on loose."

Often it seemed that we would never finish those wings, but the time came when we did. And what a job it had been (or so I, not being a craftsman, thought). Rebuilding the four wings and two ailerons, painting them with oil, then with dope-resisting paint; covering, sewing and taping them; applying three coats of P.D.N. 12, doping on serrated tape, then four coats of V.84; fitting the automatic slots, replacing the fixtures and fittings for struts, rigging-wires and aileron controls. But at last the overhauled motor was back in place, the fuselage beautifully enamelled inside and out, the floats as carefully painted, with ninety-six new screw-threads scoured out through their manhole rims; the wings loosely assembled in pairs ready to fix to the fuselage, the bent float-boom repaired with a steel sleeve, and the bruised longerons strengthened with steel fishplates. . . .

The ground outside the cargo shed had now become an island meeting-place, and some volunteers carried the float undercarriage over to some bags of sand laid on the uneven turf. Others carried out the fuselage with motor in place, the floats were lifted and tediously secured to the fuselage by thirty-six bolts and twelve bracing-wires. The next task was to level the fuselage accurately for rigging the plane. I thought this would be an easy one, but I was wrong. With great difficulty we wedged the floats up on the sandbag foundation. Millimetre by millimetre, with here a wedge and there a wedge till the spirit-level proved the fuselage to be level laterally. Then we worked to get head and tail level, but by that time one side was higher than the other. By the time the sides were level, the ends were out of true. And when the ends were level, the sides were out again. But at last, after exasperating failure for an hour and a half the plane seemed level all round. I heaved a sigh of relief and thought it a fine job until I happened to turn the spirit-level end for end. The bubble immediately rushed up it like a balloon trailing up Mount Everest! Nor could I find an accurately level level on the island. This was a difficulty I was mighty puzzled to overcome until I thought that by using the same level the same way on both plane and rigging it would make no difference if it were out of true because as far as the aeroplane was concerned it really would not know the difference.

Next we attached the wings and I was face to face with the job of rigging them. Whenever I had seen a rigger at work true-ing up the wings of a plane, I had always watched the mystic ritual in the same awed silence in which I should watch a Druid preparing a victim for sacrifice. I studied the book. The wings, it said, must be dihedrally rigged $3\frac{1}{2}°$ upwards, correct to 10' of angle and measured with a variable inclinometer. In other words, must be cocked up at the tips; but when I asked several men to lend me their variable inclinometer, they looked positively shocked as if it were an improper demand.

"Well, Roly," I said, "you'll have to make an inclinometer."

"All right," he said, "I'll make one if you can draw one."

So I marked an angle of $3\frac{1}{2}°$ on a piece of wood with my little celluloid protractor, and drew it out to three feet long. Roly took it home and planed it down till it was a long thin wedge, making a solid angle of $3\frac{1}{2}°$ at the point. His work was so accurate that I could not find the slightest deviation from the true anywhere. A fixed inclinometer was made. This we laid along the wing-spar with the level on top again. Then cocked up the wing by adjustment of the rigging-wires until the bubble was in the center of the level. Whereupon the wing must be cocked at an angle of $3\frac{1}{2}°$ with the horizontal as though about to be raised above the plane's back like the wings of a hawk about to settle. We also used our inclinometer laid across the wing to cant the leading-edge above the trailing-edge until the wing made an angle of $3\frac{1}{2}°$ with the horizontal this way also. "Stagger" was another thing we rigged for. This word was probably introduced to aerodynamics by some gentleman in the habit of finding his way home by dead-reckoning after a late night with the boys. For a stagger of $3\frac{1}{2}$ inches would imply that his upper wings were coming along $3\frac{1}{2}$ inches ahead of his lower wings.

At the finish the rigging appeared to have been so simple that I found myself looking all round the plane for something else to do which must have been forgotten. But apart from adjusting the control-cables to make the ailerons droop a quarter of an inch each side, there seemed to be only tedious little odd jobs left. And by lunch time next day the plane was finished. By Jove! She looked grand to me—superb—and handsome too, with her white enamelled body and floats, her bright aluminum wings with Kirby's jet-black lettering. . . . She was ready for launching.

I jumped her up to two-hundred feet and trimmed the elevators for hands-off flying. I left the stick alone—she flew with wings dead level. Ha! so the Lord Howe Island rigging was perfect first shot! By Jove! By *Jove!* Then the thrill of flight ran riot in me. Was it the sense of power? Controlling with scarcely an effort that hurtling, dangerous projectile. Or the thrill of the artist expressing his mood, with the air a perfect canvas, smooth, still, with no unevenness, yet with firm texture for the seaplane to grip—no floppy, thin, tropical air, this. With a slight movement of wrist—stick between thumb and finger as though it were a brush—the seaplane swept a broad stroke across the lagoon. I drew back the stick—smoothly and unhurried it seemed, yet the plane had curled upwards like a flicker of flame painted on the air; a swirl—she was round on a wing-tip and headed back over her course quicker than the artist could flourish his brush. Another twist—no more than needed to paint a curved line, and the plane had swept, and boldly drawn, the length of the lagoon beach, a man's height above it, and—sss! had rounded the rocks where the pink crab must be bubbling with rage at this strange intruder. Stick firmly pressed to one side, she had rocked on to the other wing-tip and curved round the promontory; zoom! had shot vertically upwards to jump the cargo shed; plop! had dropped back to flatten out just above the lagoon surface; roar! had darted straight at the hill behind the scene of her wreck; phut! had flattened out against the precipitous hill face, at the last moment twisting sideways, float-bottoms nearly brushing tree tops; had turned about, floats within a few inches of the surface, motor roaring at full throttle, to shoot straight at Goat Island, and—zip! at the last moment hurdled the island with a laugh from me at young Dignam on the top ducking behind a rock. Ha! ha! what sport in the world could touch this? *Elijah* rioted in her new life; now she was a bird and threw her weight about the sky like a wild, mad plover. Sweeping up till she stood on her tail, and as she lost way, toppling over sideways as though shot, to drop dead for 500 feet till the wires screamed in the wind, and I reached, through fierce exhilaration, an ecstatic consciousness of vital power; while blood and flesh strove and fought against the startling acceleration of being hurled earthwards. Beautiful plane! Amazing *Elijah!* Returned to such life as she never had before. . . .

PART V

Your Dangerous Freedom

THE PLANE
by Sidney Alexander

A paradoxical December afternoon
when Spring with little breasts crept into
Winter's cold sheets and lingered for a day—
From where we stood on our high stoop, the little park—
so scrawny-green in the slum—tinkled
with bright arpeggios of children's shouts:
dancing with joy more dismal adult moods
till gloom, ludicrous as balloons, exploded
in the scintillating skirts and body-whirl,
glowing our faces like the pretzel-man
who wheeled his little carriage by the rail.

And then above the greenish-blue horizon
I saw that speck, innocent as Maypoles danced around,
yet at its sight the blue flesh of the sky
no longer pulsed soft to the bachelor eye.
What was it? bird? or chimney-soot?
or kite of invisible boy above the roofs?
What thing had come from behind the water's edge?
What was that scratch etched on the plate-gray sky?
and now the scratch had split . . . and now two wings
and from nowhere and everywhere vibrating in the blood
a hum organic as the pulse of fear. . . .

Why don't you run? you child with eyes like flashing mirrors?
the plane is roaring toward . . . why don't you hide
now in the blessed interval? there still is time!
and you, John, unemployed, fing'ring the furry bud,
quick! flat on face! or delve in subway mouth!
the plane is roaring toward . . . lord over us
lord over you and me and all our insect ways
lord over laughter and our tangled skein of dream
lord over what we are and what we seem
the plane is overhead . . .

                   then like a curse
to keep imprisoned in my eyes bright bowl,
back back I bent my head until the world
had dropped as shoreline below rail—and held that plane:
cleaving the air while small beneath its struts
a bird raced with that buzzing speck of steel:
that flying motor: the man sitting upon it
goggled and blinking in the airy crests,
and I and the dancing child and the fat balloons
mere perforations on a film that reeled
beneath his wing—the winds thru wires rushing—
I saw that angel of Icarus, shrouded in the fog,
minister bright love of exploding petals
on streets of Madrid—and sandy geysers fell—

The plane was gone
but suddenly the sky's blue canopy had sagged:
the poles kicked over: the smiling tent gashed:
the air sharp with flying knives
the afternoon hanging down in shreds
and only a brute leer grinning across the sky
horizon to horizon darkening us—

[110]

I remember the children laughed when it went over
and pointed at the sky. And someone yawned.
yet hanging in the air
the high unbearable harmonic of our fear—
O what shall we say to those who ride in planes?
we who breathe in the intervals of bombs?
we ground-moles crawling between the crackling borders?
we whose boundaries are the backs of electric cats?
what rising gusts of our youth shall send us spinning
in flickers of sun-spokes there in the highest reaches
airwashed and clean as songs of birds unpinioned!

Entries from "Journal of an Airman"
by W. H. Auden

My mother's dislike of my uncle, the people's satisfaction at crashes. "If the Lord had intended people to fly He'd have given them wings," compared with their day-dreams of looping the loop, the falling leaf, dragging their chum from blazing fuselage —signs of a mixed character. Most people mixed characters—the two-faced, the obscure and amazed, the touch-line admirers.

Note.—The aeroplane has only recently become necessary, owing to the progress of enemy propaganda, and even now not for flying itself, but as a guarantee of good faith to the people, frightened by ghost stories, the enemy's distorted vision of the airman's activities.

The Airman's Alphabet

ACE—
Pride of parents
and photographed person
and laughter in leather.

BOMB—
Curse from cloud
and coming to crook
and saddest to steeple.

COCKPIT—
Soft seat
and support of soldier
and hold for hero.

DEATH—   Award for wildness
             and worst in the west
             and painful to pilots.

ENGINE—   Darling of designers
             and dirty dragon
             and revolving roarer.

FLYING—   Habit of hawks
             and unholy hunting
             and ghostly journey.

GAUGE—   Informer about oil
             and important to eye
             and graduated glass.

HANGAR—   Mansion of machine
             and motherly to metal
             and house of handshaking.

INSTRUMENT— Dial on dashboard
             and destroyer of doubt
             and father of fact.

JOYSTICK—   Pivot of power
             and responder to pressure
             and grip for the glove.

KISS—   Touch taking off
             and tenderness in time
             and firmness on flesh.

LOOPING—   Flying folly
             and feat at fairs
             and brave to boys.

MECHANIC—   Owner of overalls
and interested in iron
and trusted with tools.

NOSE-DIVE—   Nightmare to nerves
and needed by no one
and dash toward death.

OBSERVER—   Peeper through periscope
and peerer at pasture
and eyes in the air.

PROPELLER—   Wooden wind-oar
and twisted whirler
and lifter of load.

QUIET—   Absent from airmen
and easy to horses
and got in the grave.

RUDDER—   Deflector of flight
and flexible fin
and pointer of path.

STORM—   Night from the north
and numbness nearing
and hail ahead.

TIME—   Expression of alarm
and used by the ill
and personal space.

UNDERCARRIAGE— Softener of shock
and seat on the soil
and easy to injure.

VICTIM—   Corpse after crash
             and carried through country
             and atonement for aircraft.

WIRELESS—   Sender of signal
             and speaker of sorrow
             and news from nowhere.

X—   Mark upon map
             and meaning mischief
             and lovers' lingo.

YOUTH—   Daydream of devils
             and dear to the damned
             and always to us.

ZERO—   Love before leaving
             and touch of terror
             and time of attack.

Three signs of an airman—practical jokes—nervousness before taking off—rapid healing after injury.

Of the Enemy—

>   His collar was spotless; he talked very well,
>   He spoke of our homes and duty and we fell.

Three kinds of enemy walk—the grandiose stunt—the melancholic stagger—the paranoiac sidle.

Three kinds of enemy bearing—the condor stoop—the toad stupor—the robin's stance.

Three kinds of enemy face—the June bride—the favourite puss—the stone in the rain.

Three kinds of enemy eye—the lobster—the boot-button—the submarine.

Three kinds of enemy hand—the marsh—the claw—the dead yam.

Three kinds of enemy clothing—fisherman's pockets—Dickens' waistcoats—adhesive trousers.

Three enemy traits—refusal to undress in public—proficiency in modern languages—inability to travel back to the engine.

Three enemy occupations—playing cards—collecting—talking to animals.

Three terms of enemy speech—I mean—quite frankly—speaking as a scientist, etc.

Three signs of an enemy letter—underlining—parentheses in brackets—careful obliteration of cancelled expressions.

Three enemy questions—Am I boring you?—Could you tell me the time?—Are you sure you're fit enough?

Three enemy catchwords—insure now—keep smiling—safety first.

Three enemy don'ts—don't kiss your baby on the mouth—don't lean out of the carriage window—don't miss this.

Three signs of an enemy country—licensed hours—a national art—nursery schools.

Three signs of an enemy house—old furniture—a room called the Den—photographs of friends.

Three warnings of enemy attack—depression in the mornings—rheumatic twinges—blips on the face.

Three symptoms in convalescence—nail-biting—nightmares—short-sight.

Three results of an enemy victory—impotence—cancer—paralysis.

Three counter attacks—complete mastery of the air—ancestor worship—practical jokes.

MESSAGE RECEIVED
by Sonia Raiziss

ITEM: A war pigeon released into storm was admitted
lost. For three days and three nights it fought through
weather and death and then found home.

Tag him, forward him gently home:
His homing eyes had best remember.
Clear weather, blizzard below.
Embrace him with soft means and facile temper,
Use him for these ungracious ends,
Released now under the whole clear dome
Of world; let mercury go.

The wind admits no foes, no friends
In weather wars, campaigns of painted rags,
Clash of coins, blue books, talk tags.
The wind shall tear the bloodwashed, the rainblack
Shirt off any man's back
And snap white sheets from the white book
For the history of last oblivion.

Carry his tender feathers, hawk, and look,
Vampire bird, to your overgrown wings;
Platinum claws, unpinion
The anxious dove: routes remembering, things
Remembered—never yours.

[117]

Nor has the storm an ear for wars.
Clear weather, blizzard below.

Who knows: heaven can be too high.
But not your partisan technic, not your miracle
Convoyed such messenger beyond cold hell,
One pigeon plunging with plummet eye
Through dark, through day. Three days: prodigal
Redeemed: and they at the homecoming know.
Clear weather, quiet carrion below.

SKY WRITERS
by William Rose Benét

. . . In graceful windings, trailing their white exhaust,
The insect planes—as a window is furred by frost—
Wrote on the sky, and the scales fell from our eyes
And to us was revealed—that It Pays to Advertise.

As the radio erupts with some eunuch voice
Bidding us in a breakfast food rejoice,
So the writing upon the sky as it drifts and thins,
Tremendously imparts—a bargain in skins.

The mouths gaped; the eyes bulged; head after head
Twisted skyward; the lips moved and read. . . .
And I saw the mountains fallen, the world's foundations fled,
And the sky rolled up like a scroll for a judgement on the dead.

The Aviator
by Alexander Blok
(*Translated by Payson Loomis*)

The plane, released, its twin blades waving,
Like ocean monster from the shore
Slipping to sea, slides forth ascending
Upon the currents of the air.

Like strings the song of the propeller.
And look: the pilot resolute
Towards the blind sun above the grandstand
Pursues the spiral of his flight.

Now at a height unknown, undreamt of,
The metal of the rudder gleams;
There the invisible propeller,
Still audible, still faintly hums.

And then—in vain the eye seeks further:
On all the vacant sky no trace:
Up-turned binoculars show merely
Air clear as water, empty space.

And here where crawling mist envelops
The hangars in the quivering heat,

The field, the people, all the earthly
As though to prostrate earth pressed flat.

Now from the golden fog emerging
A ghostly chord rolls in and grows.
He is there! He has broken the record!
A burst of murmurous applause.

Lower, lower the downward spiral,
Steeper the inward-curving streak,
And suddenly—in even rhythm
A clumsy and unrhythmic break. . . .

Hangs at a terrifying angle
A beast with huge antennae stayed. . . .
Seek, seek thou with thine eyes gone sightless
A buttress in the air—the void!

Now is too late: from the grass glistens
A wing's unmoving, crumpled end;
Among the tangled struts projecting,
And deader than the stick, a hand.

Why on this first and final venture,
O bold one, didst thou brave the skies?
—That some spoiled mercenary beauty
Turn skyward her ecstatic eyes?

Or didst thou know the fierce destructive
Rapture of self-oblivion,
And, craving doom, shut off the motor
By uncontrollable design?

Or did some spectrous apparition
Of wars to come dissolve thy sight:
Planes in the ⌐urk of night unloading
Earthwards their gifts of dynamite?

1910

A Sonnet to Orpheus
by Rainer Maria Rilke
(*Translated by M. D. Herter Norton*)

O not till the time when flight
no longer will mount for its own sake
into the sky stillnesses,
sufficient unto itself,

that in luminous profilings,
as the tool that succeeded,
it may play the winds' favorite,
surely curving and slim—

not till a pure Whither
outweighs boyish pride
of growing machines,

will the one who, headlong with winning,
has drawn near the distances,
be his lone flight's attaining.

PART VI

The Hawk Without a Hood

The War in Heaven
by John Milton

Now storming fury rose,
And clamour such as heard in Heav'n till now
Was never. Arms on Armour clashing bray'd
Horrible discord, and the madding Wheeles
Of brazen Chariots rag'd; dire was the noise
Of conflict; over head the dismal hiss
Of fiery Darts in flaming volies flew,
And flying vaulted either Host with fire.
So under fierie Cope together rush'd
Both Battels maine, with ruinous assault
And inextinguishable rage; all Heav'n
Resounded, and had Earth bin then, all Earth
Had to her Center shook. What wonder? when
Millions of fierce encountring Angels fought
On either side, the least of whom could weild
These Elements, and arm him with the force
Of all thir Regions: how much more of Power
Armie against Armie numberless to raise
Dreadful combustion warring, and disturb,
Though not destroy, thir happie Native seat;
Had not th'Eternal King Omnipotent
From his strong hold of Heav'n high over-rul'd
And limited thir might; though numberd such
As each divided Legion might have seemed

A numerous Host, in strength each armed hand
A Legion; led in fight, yet Leader seemd
Each Warrior single as in Chief, expert
When to advance, or stand, or turn the sway
Of Battel, open when, and when to close
The ridges of grim Warr; no thought of flight,
None of retreat, no unbecoming deed
That argu'd fear; each on himself reli'd,
As onely in his arm the moment lay
Of victorie; deeds of eternal fame
Were don, but infinite: for wide was spred
That Warr and various; somtimes on firm ground
A standing fight, then soaring on main wing
Tormented all the Air; all Air seemd then
Conflicting Fire: long time in even scale
The Battel hung; till *Satan* who that day
Prodigious power had shewn, and met in Armes
No equal, raunging through the dire attack
Of fighting Seraphim confus'd, at length,
Saw where the Sword of *Michael* smote, and fell'd
Squadrons at once, with huge two-handed sway
Brandisht aloft the horrid edge came down
Wide wasting; such destruction to withstand
He hasted, and oppos'd the rockie Orb
Of tenfold Adamant, his ample Shield
A vast circumference: At his approach
The great Arch-Angel from his warlike toile
Surceas'd, and glad as hoping here to end
Intestine War in Heav'n, the arch foe subdu'd
Or Captive drag'd in Chains, with hostile frown
And visage all enflam'd first thus began.
Author of Evil, unknown till thy revolt,

Unnam'd in Heav'n, now plenteous, as thou seest
These Acts of hateful strife, hateful to all,
Though heaviest by just measure on thy self
And thy adherents: how hast thou disturb'd
Heav'ns blessed peace, and into Nature brought
Miserie, uncreated till the crime
Of thy Rebellion? how hast thou instill'd
Thy malice into thousands, once upright
And faithful, now prov'd false. But think not here
To trouble Holy Rest; Heav'n casts thee out
From all her Confines. Heav'n the seat of bliss
Brooks not the works of violence and Warr.

FLYING SCHOOL 1914
by Richard Euringer

Fischer had mounted two of the "new" L.V.G.'s. One of them had been got ready by Schwink and Sirry; the other one, that dark brown old box, which Captain Wirth had already refused to take over, was for Lieutenant Murner. It stood next to the smart L.V.G. looking like a mangy old pack camel. There was something rather touching about it. We tapped all its parts, inside and out. A home must be found for it somewhere. Someone will crash in it, but anyway it will turn up again at No. 4 School, having passed in due course through Schools 1 to 3.

At that time—the period following on November 10, the front seemed to be actually heaving under the devastating gun-fire. Pilots understood none of the details of what was happening, but the observers suddenly had an important air. Divisional headquarters wanted to keep a tighter hand on the pilots, and so the squadron was soon on the move. With our workshop, four hangars, and the greater part of the men, the squadron commander set out to find a little château. It was pouring with rain, and those days made us familiar with Flanders mist. Two machines were smashed up. Clods of mud flew around the cockpit; the tyres stuck to the earth. We stood about stamping in the mud, but the mist would not sink, and would not rise. The squadron commander sent us the ominous message that he had found a château . . . that was late in the evening. During the night the mist cleared before a gale. Towards midnight the stars shone out clearly, but the driving clouds passed in close formation across the sky above a burning village. Two hours later the tent-poles were bending, as the storm drove the clouds along. Meteorologically it was uncanny. The Prussians turned the men out. As the wind was tugging at the tent-pegs, there was a risk that the tent might fly away. That night a couple of grapnels were pulled up. The heavy planes bellied and flapped whenever a bit of canvas slipped open. The wind howled and whistled round the entrenchments. In the morning Captain Brauer's anemometer registered something unbelievable. Impatience produced a sinking feeling in our stomachs. It was difficult to imagine just what would happen if a plane were to attempt to fight against the storm. If the propeller should jam, as it whirled about the clods of earth, one would be hurled by the gale against the ramparts and then whirled along like a scrap of paper, whipped by the wind.

There was a roaring and a shaking; the rage of the bombardment made such a savage accompaniment to the soughing of the trees and the fury of the upper elements, that we found ourselves suffering from acute pains in the stomach. After one such interlude two men of the squadron to which we were attached opened a tent and pushed their machines out. . . . Did they really intend to fly? When one gives the lead, others usually follow it!

Was a lead necessary? Ungewitter ran to get his helmet and rifle. I shouted after him: "Bring my helmet and coat . . ." My voice did not carry. A man ran after him.

If the Prussians had a shot at it, why not others?

Men hung on to all the struts. The roar of the propellers was drowned in the gale. Men struggled to hold the planes down and rammed pegs into the ground.

Prussians have always taken the lead, and others have followed. It needed no special skill to stagger along right behind them. Besides, we knew now what was up. I had been at the High Command on the evening before the battle. Crown Prince Rupprecht was standing there, very pale. Though only a junior officer, I had gathered that if we were now held up the winter weather would prevent any further progress. In the East the Russians were moving in enormous numbers into our country. Ungewitter did not return. I sent some men after him, who reported that he was engaged with the artillery commander.

The first machine hardly moved along the ground, for the hurricane lifted her over the trees. The wind shrieked in the fuselage, but the machine made no progress forward, she only went higher. Mysteriously she shot up, a thing without weight, and hung as though attached by ropes, her propeller digging into the air, while the next machine followed hard on her track. Then I saw no more. Savagely the storm tore at the tent. Ungewitter staggered up, threw me my gear, and shouted that the skipper had telephoned he was being pressed by Divisional H.Q.: Couldn't we fly? He had reported it was impossible. What did we think about it?

To that there could be but one answer.

One machine came down again. That didn't matter to us now.

As that machine was being stowed away, Captain Brauer came along and signed to give it up. With a neck-breaking, gull-like action he trundled the other machine into the open space and pancaked.

"That's finished it!" shouted Brauer. "We'll only crash."

If he'd come up to us and lifted us out of the cockpit I should probably have been grateful to him. It would have been a back door through which we could have slipped with some kind of decency. But, as it was, he merely said: "I have forbidden you gentlemen to go up."

And our skipper asked us what we thought.

To that I found no reply.

So we staggered up. It was not pleasant. But after five frightful minutes we knew at any rate that it was feasible. The Prussians had made it possible, and my old box stood it; that ancient contraption, which was like a silver fish with its frosted aluminum cockpit. We sang wild songs of rage and defiance at the storm. The citadel whirled away below us. It was more dangerous to plane down than to fight one's way right through to the more stable layers of the air.

The enormous Ypres salient was spread out below under a haze of the smoke from the guns. Dark fragments of cloud, like cottonwood whales, surged at us, 600 metres off. We topped them, gleaming white over the swollen shadows, while they dragged across the map of the landscape. We had to drop Verey lights over Warneton. Warneton lay somewhere below. That old bus knew how to jump about. After 1,200 metres the grey mist suddenly disappeared for a few moments and a gleam of daylight showed through the uncertain darkness. I pressed on upwards; over the massed clouds, out of the haze of streaming mist into the elemental hurricane. When at 1,600 metres the rainbow gloriole of the propeller rose from the waving cloudscapes into the glacial blue of the clearer zone, a couple of shell cloudlets, fired at random, floated in the air quite prettily, but neither eye nor field-glasses could pierce the cloudbank, whose brilliant surface contrasted with the murky flashes of gun-fire.

Francis kept waving his map and gesticulating: we were too comfortable; it was no good, we had to go through the "snow" again. . . . As, with an invocation to the deity, I dashed at the next cloudbank, we saw our own plane rushing at us rainbow-hued. Then we were swallowed in the darkness. . . .

For an hour we laboured; we revelled in lift sensations. I had only one anxiety, that my friend with the meteorological name would fall out. He did indeed drop his sixteen-pointed star on to the fighting ant-heap below, but—truth to tell—we had not much to show for our labour. We swooped and planed; the storm buffeted us, but the battle owed us nothing on that day of wind and danger, November 12.

Checkmated, we returned home. Home behind Comines and Warneton, in a toy château, surrounded by waving elms, set in a park.

Damnation! What we wanted was a landing-place!

I was beginning to feel angry.

We banked steeply downwards, setting our teeth. There was not a patch to land on. Only a narrow strip of rough ploughed land between the park and the stunted willows. The gale was behind us. We planed down. (It seemed to me that the head wind counterbalanced the weight of the machine.) A gust from the flank pushed the tail of the machine down towards the branches; trees drifted by.

The bus slipped along an avenue with elms on the right, stunted willows on the left; caught, broke away, soared upwards, banked again with the wind behind, and sheered off again for the ploughfield, a mere strip of molehills between the park and the willows.

I saw the danger and understood what was happening. But I was no longer interested as to exactly how I should land in front of the château.

With a kind of malicious joy I realised what was going to happen. . . . The left wing brushed the tree-tops and crumpled up like a paper bag. With a sudden windmill action the machine swerved and the tail went up, straight in the air like the fin of a whale. I saw a broken branch rushing at my left goggle, close to the eye. The glass smashed. I laughed. My eye was saved! Cautiously, I opened my eye.

I never felt the landing. The machine dived straight down into the brambles with a force that buried the motor right up to the third cylinder. For long afterwards I heard the crashing and splintering of framework, fuselage and branches. My belt was torn as we bumped, and I was thrown head downwards into the brambles. Wedged between the motor and the tank, I hung there, head downwards. I felt very sick.

Men rushed up with picks and shovels and began the work of extricating us. Suddenly there was a piercing yell. Francis wanted to curse but couldn't think of anything to say. He collapsed exhausted on top of me, his legs dangling behind him.

In their eagerness to get him free they had sawed at his ankles. He was moaning at the loss of his left leg.

I lost my Francis. They packed him off home. I gave him his little Iron Cross in hospital (for a rifle encounter with two British Bristols). Afterwards he became an accomplished pilot.

What about the machine? It was an extraordinary sight. The carriage was the only thing on it that hadn't lost any parts. It stretched its wheels up in to the air. Perhaps the same wheels that you admired on the old flounder here. No, those are rubber tyres. Perhaps the axle was the same, if it hasn't been repeatedly smashed up since then. They attached new wings, antediluvian in all conscience, made up of God knows what old patches of linen. The old belt had been torn away—the one that almost burst my stomach muscles—but it had been given a new belt. No scrap of linen, no cable, strut, beam, spar, nut, bolt or screw survived, but by some miracle it was the same machine.

The old flounder nursed a great secret. It was a giant ship

but a very short time ago. Someone cut out a bloodstained piece of cloth and worked on it the number 4. There it lay, felled, but not dead, a memorial; its own War memorial.

L.G.V.—B.43 . . . old tin Lizzie! My black-brown flounder. It was an old box, but the old box was new. Not a patch of the original was left after all its crashes. And the machine was there still.

Get your knees around it, my dear Murner, pack yourself into the new machine, which is your first, and solve the mystery! Between heaven and earth, spinning as though to crash, man and machine together; you will then understand the miracle of flight.

AN IRISH AIRMAN FORESEES HIS DEATH
by W. B. Yeats

I know that I shall meet my fate
Somewhere among the clouds above;
Those that I fight I do not hate,
Those that I guard I do not love;
My country is Kiltartan Cross,
My countrymen Kiltartan's poor,
No likely end could bring them loss
Or leave them happier than before.
Nor law, nor duty bade me fight,
Nor public men, nor cheering crowds,
A lonely impulse of delight
Drove to this tumult in the clouds;
I balanced all, brought all to mind,
The years to come seem waste of breath,
A waste of breath the years behind
In balance with this life, this death.

SAGITTARIUS RISING
by Cecil Lewis

SQUADRONS UP, 1914

At last, after a month's preparation, the squadron was ready. The machines were lined up by Flights in front of the sheds, three rows of four each. They looked very imposing. The February sun glistened on their new white wings. The streamers fluttered from the rudders of the Flight-Commanders. The Lewis guns stood cocked up on their mountings. The pilots and observers, muffled up in their leather coats, stumped about in their sheepskin boots, strapping up their haversacks, looking over their machines, polishing their goggles. They collected round the Major for final instructions, consulted their maps, and then went off, pulling on flying-caps and mufflers, climbed into their cockpits and strapped themselves in. The mechanics kicked the chocks more firmly against the wheels and sucked in the engines. Contact! The pilots spun their starting magnetos, and one by one the engines sprung into life. Three minutes to warm them up, and then a heavy roar, which rose and fell as pilot after pilot ran up his engine, tested his magnetos, and then, satisfied, throttled down again. At last they were all ready, engines ticking over, and a deep thrumming of the planes and wires vibrating filled the air. The Major dropped his hand, and a Flight-Commander opened his engine up, turned, and taxied away down the aerodrome. The others followed him, single file, and one by one they headed to the wind, pushed their throttles open, rose, swaying in the ground gusts, and sailed up towards the sheds.

We stood on the tarmac watching them go. And still, after twenty years, my heart swells at the memory of the sight. I can hear the strong engines and smell the tang of the burnt oil. I can see them as they came hurtling up, their goggled pilots and observers leaning down to wave a last farewell before they passed in a deafening flash of speed and smoke fifty feet overhead. One by one they came up as if saluting us—drum roll crescendo, cymbal crash, rapid diminuendo. One by one they disappeared behind the sheds.

It was a prelude to action in that noble and tragic adventure of the world's youth; the first visible instance of collective farewell; the first realization of a grim purpose behind that casual and carefree life. It caught at my heart then, as a stage show catches its audience, which weeps, almost with pleasure, at the tragedy of others; which shares, at a remove, an agony it need not undergo. I was an onlooker that day; they were a symbol of the time: young men who rose up, passed with a cry and a gesture, and were gone. When my turn came I did not feel it so.

Once in the air, the squadron took formation. The three flights, each a diamond (Flight-Commander leading, numbers two and three to right and left, fifty yards between wing-tips, number four a hundred yards directly behind the leader and slightly above to avoid his slipstream), wheeled, a moving arrowhead (A Flight leading, B and C to right and left), over the green fields and the white cliffs of England, passed majestically away in the sunlight, growing smaller and smaller as they climbed, the roar of their engines sinking to a murmur, and the murmur dying to silence before we lost them. At last, straining our eyes, we could see them no longer. They were twelve remote and splendid spirits who had gone.

The squadron sets out eleven strong on the evening patrol. Eleven chocolate-colored, lean, noisy bullets, lifting, swaying, turning, rising into formation—two fours and a three—circling and climbing away steadily towards the lines. They are off to deal with Richthofen and his circus of Red Albatrosses.

The May evening is heavy with threatening masses of cumulus cloud, majestic skyscapes, solid-looking as snow mountains, fraught with caves and valleys, rifts and ravines—strange and secret pathways in the chartless continents of the sky. Below, the land becomes an ordnance map, dim green and yellow, and across it go the Lines, drawn anyhow, as a child might scrawl with a double pencil. The grim dividing Lines! From the air robbed of all significance.

Steadily the body of scouts rises higher and higher, threading its way between the cloud precipices. Sometimes, below, the streets of a village, the corner of a wood, a few dark figures moving, glides into view like a slide into a lantern and then is hidden again.

But the fighting pilot's eyes are not on the ground, but roving endlessly through the lower and higher reaches of the sky, peering anxiously through fur-goggles to spot those black slow-moving specks against land or cloud which mean full throttle, tense muscles, held breath, and the headlong plunge with screaming wires—a Hun * in the sights, and the tracers flashing.

A red light curls up from the leader's cockpit and falls away. Action! He alters direction slightly, and the patrol, shifting throttle and rudder, keep close like a pack of hounds on the scent. He has seen, and they see soon, six scouts three thousand

---

* It has been suggested that this word has an ugly connotation, and that I should not use it. But we always referred to our friends the enemy as "Huns," just as the Infantry knew them as "Fritz" or "Jerry," and nothing derogatory was, or is, intended. . . .

feet below. Black crosses! It seems interminable till the eleven come within diving distance. The pilots nurse their engines, hard-minded and set, test their guns and watch their indicators. At last the leader sways sideways, as a signal that each should take his man, and suddenly drops.

Machines fall scattering, the earth races up, the enemy patrol, startled, wheels and breaks. Each his man! The chocolate thunderbolts take sights, steady their screaming planes, and fire. A burst, fifty rounds—it is over. They have overshot, and the enemy, hit or missed, is lost for the moment. The pilot steadies his stampeding mount, pulls her out with a firm hand, twisting his head right and left, trying to follow his man, to sight another, to back up a friend in danger, to note another in flames.

But the squadron plunging into action had not seen, far off, approaching from the east, the rescue flight of Red Albatrosses patrolling above the body of machines on which they had dived, to guard their tails and second them in the battle. These, seeing the maze of wheeling machines, plunge down to join them. The British scouts, engaging and disengaging like flies circling at midday in a summer room, soon find the newcomers upon them. Then, as if attracted by some mysterious power, as vultures will draw to a corpse in the desert, other bodies of machines swoop down from the peaks of the cloud mountains. More enemy scouts, and, by good fortune, a flight of Naval Triplanes.

But, nevertheless, the enemy, double in number, greater in power and fighting with skill and courage, gradually overpower the British, whose machines scatter, driven down beneath the scarlet German fighters.

It would be impossible to describe the action of such a battle. A pilot, in the second between his own engagements, might see a Hun diving vertically, an SE 5 on his tail, on the tail of the SE another Hun, and above him again another British scout.

These four, plunging headlong at two hundred miles an hour, guns crackling, tracers streaming, suddenly break up. The lowest Hun plunges flaming to his death, if death has not taken him already. His victor seems to stagger, suddenly pulls out in a great leap, as a trout leaps on the end of a line, and then, turning over on his belly, swoops and spins in a dizzy falling spiral with the earth to end it. The third German zooms veering, and the last of that meteoric quartet follows bursting. . . . But such a glimpse, lasting perhaps ten seconds, is broken by the sharp rattle of another attack. Two machines approach head-on at breakneck speed, firing at each other, tracers whistling through each other's planes, each slipping sideways on his rudder to trick the other's gunfire. Who will hold longest? Two hundred yards, a hundred, fifty, and then, neither hit, with one accord they fling their machines sideways, bank and circle, each striving to bring his gun onto the other's tail, each glaring through goggle eyes, calculating, straining, wheeling, grim, bent only on death or dying.

But, from above, this strange, tormented circling is seen by another Hun. He drops. His gun speaks. The British machine, distracted by the sudden unseen enemy, pulls up, takes a burst through the engine, tank and body, and falls uppermost down through the clouds and the deep unending desolation of the twilight sky.

The game of noughts and crosses, starting at fifteen thousand feet above the clouds, drops in altitude engagement by engagement. Friends and foes are scattered. A last SE, pressed by two Huns, plunges and wheels, gun-jammed, like a snipe over marshes, darts lower, finds refuge in the ground mist, and disappears.

Now lowering clouds darken the evening. Below, flashes of gunfire stab the veil of the gathering dusk. The fight is over!

The battlefield shows no sign. In the pellucid sky, serene cloud mountains mass and move unceasingly. Here where guns rattled and death plucked the spirits of the valiant, this thing is now as if it had never been! The sky is busy with night, passive, superb, unheeding.

FLYING ALONE, 1936

Nothing gives such a sense of mastery over mechanism, mastery indeed over space, time, and life itself, as this. Most men covet the power of putting the world, their world, into perspective, of seeing themselves in relation to it, of achieving some sort of harmony with their environment. It involves mastery, for that alone gives detachment, and only from detachment comes harmony—a sense of values. Never, it seems, has the world had so poor a sense of values as today. So, if the muddleheaded idiocy of men angers and intimidates you—for though fools running about with loaded revolvers may only make you angry, their potential power for damage cannot but be frightening—if the daily manifestations of an approaching cataclysm, which mutter and shake on the four horizons, make you despair, I recommend a trip to ten thousand feet to recover your sense of values —and your sense of humor.

From such a height how insignificant the works of men's hands appear! How everything they do seems to disfigure the face of the earth; but when they have done their worst, what a lot of it is left! This curious and intricate agglomeration of little pink boxes is a city. It looks rather like an open sore in the green flesh of the earth; but not, after all, such a very large one. Left for a few hundred years it will heal up and the world will be none the worse. In contrast, how satisfying and permanent are the shapes of the woods and the pattern of the tilled and fallow fields. These are the first and last things, and will persist in the face of all conquest or defeat while any men endure. That minute cluster of weathered roofs set in the fold of the valley is a village. It looks right, as if it had grown there; it cannot be far wrong. Beyond, how ample are the courses of the rivers and the contours of the coasts! With what grace and spontaneity is the world laid out! Man-made order and precision, square, circle, or straight line, is an offense among this greater harmony, where nothing seems planned, yet all falls home just so. In truth it cannot last, this mechanical geometrical civilization of ours, for the simple and final reason that it does not *look* right. It offends the esthetic sense, and that, of all men's senses, is the most deeply rooted and changeless. So, let it go. After all, if we take a perspective in time comparable to the one we have taken in height, how mushroom-like is our scientific epoch. Two hundred years ago it was not thought of. Now it rages like a cholera epidemic. Soon, having taken its toll, it will die out, leaving us inoculated or immune. That we are doomed to live in this feverish age, rushing hither and thither, crying Lo, here! or Lo, there! like madmen in a darkened room, is our misfortune; but momentarily withdrawn from it all, sailing godlike above its clamor, comes a curious certainty: it does not matter, it will not last; the world is very foolish, but it is very young.

ALL THE DEAD PILOTS
by William Faulkner

In the pictures, the snapshots hurriedly made, a little faded, a little dog-eared with the thirteen years, they swagger a little. Lean, hard, in their brass-and-leather martial harness, posed standing beside or leaning upon the esoteric shapes of wire and wood and canvas in which they flew without parachutes, they too have an esoteric look; a look not exactly human, like that of some dim and threatful apotheosis of the race seen for an instant in the glare of a thunderclap and then forever gone.

Because they are dead, all the old pilots, dead on the eleventh of November, 1918. When you see modern photographs of them, the recent pictures made beside the recent shapes of steel and canvas with the new cowlings and engines and slotted wings, they look a little outlandish: the lean young men who once swaggered. They look lost, baffled. In this saxophone age of flying they look as out of place as, a little thick about the waist, in the sober business suits of thirty and thirty-five and perhaps more than that, they would look among the saxophones and miniature brass bowlers of a night club orchestra. Because they are dead too, who had learned to respect that whose respect in turn their hardness had commanded before there were welded center sections and parachutes and ships that would not spin. That's why they watch the saxophone girls and boys with slip-stream-proof lipstick and aeronautical flasks piling up the saxophone crates in private driveways and on golf greens, with the

[143]

quick sympathy and the bafflement too. "My gad," one of them—
ack emma, warrant officer pilot, captain and M.C. in turn—said
to me once, "if you can treat a crate that way, why do you want
to fly at all?"

But they are all dead now. They are thick men now, a little
thick about the waist from sitting behind desks, and maybe not
so good at it, with wives and children in suburban homes almost
paid out, with gardens in which they putter in the long eve-
nings after the 5:15 is in, and perhaps not so good at that either:
the hard, lean men who swaggered hard and drank hard because they had found that being dead was not as quiet as they
had heard it would be. That's why this story is composite: a
series of brief glares in which, instantaneous and without depth
or perspective, there stood into sight the portent and the threat
of what the race could bear and become, in an instant between
dark and dark.

* * *

The Air Raid
by Archibald MacLeish

The Announcer
They follow each other like footsteps.
The steel stamps on the sky: the
Heel hits. . . .
                They hang like
Quills driven in sky:—
The quarry invisible . . .
       (*An explosion is clearly heard.*)
                  Nearer. . . .
     (*The police whistle blows sharply. Under the voices the
       explosions are always louder. Under the explosions the
       inaudible vibration of many planes swells painfully into
       heavy suffocating sound.*)

The Voice of the Sergeant
You can hear for yourselves! You will now follow the orders—
To occupy the vaults of village churches:
In any event to descend from upper floors and
Scatter in streets avoiding visible gatherings. . . .

Women's Voices
They're coming.
         I hear them.
               They're nearer.

A Girl's Voice (*frightened*)

They're nearer! They're nearer!

A Woman's Voice
Ah they'll go over. There's nothing to fear: they'll go over.
They always do: they go over. Don't you fear.
Don't you fret. Don't you peer in the air—they'll
Go. They will. You'll forget they were ever by Saturday.

The Old Woman's Voice
Dukes: Kings: Emperors—now there's this kind.
They're all fools—the lot of them: always were:
Marching around with their drums: shooting their guns off!
Let them step till they stop if it gives them pleasure.
It's all one to us if they do or they don't.
We needn't crick our necks to watch it . . .

> (*The roar of the planes increases in slow oppressive crescendo. The explosions are no longer heard.*)

The Announcer
We hear them: we can't see them.

We hear the shearing metal:
We hear the tearing air.

All we see is sun.

Sun: the hawk's ambush.

Their flight is from the sun.

They might be low: they might be
Well down—three thousand.

They might be less.
They are many:
Hard to guess how many. . . .
(*rapidly*)
We've got them now: we see them:
They're out of the dazzle: they're flying
Fighting formation in column
Squadron following squadron
Ten—fifteen squadrons
Bombing models mostly
Big ones: three motors. . . .

Not so low as we figured them. . . .

Almost over. . . .
(*The roar of the planes breaks: rises sharply in pitch:
diminishes: the women's voices above it.*)
WOMEN'S VOICES
Look!

Look! Look! Look!

THE ANNOUNCER (*rapidly*)
They're changing formation they're banking
The whole flight is banking
Front wheeling to flank
Flank anchored and climbing
Climbing bank into line. . . .

The line swung like a lariat!

WOMEN'S VOICES
Look! It's circling as a bird does!

[147]

It circles as a hawk would circle hunting!

It's hunting us under the roof: the room: the curtain!

THE ANNOUNCER
They're wheeling round for the town
They're rounding in by the river
They're giving it throttle they're climbing
The timing is perfect they're flying with
Perfect precision of timing
Perfect mechanical certainty. . . .

WOMEN'S VOICES
Show it our skirts!
                    Show it our shawls!
All of us: into the street all of us!

THE ANNOUNCER
They turn like stones on a string:
They swing like steel in a groove:
They move like tools not men:
You'd say there were no men:
You'd say they had no will but the
Will of motor on metal. . . .
        (*The roar of the planes increases from moment to mo-
        ment.*)

WOMEN'S VOICES
Show it our skirts in the street: it won't hurt us!

Show it our softness! Show it our weakness!

Show it our womanhood!

[148]

Into the street!

Into the street all of us!
>*(The pitch of the roar opens: the sound is huge, brutal, close.)*

THE ANNOUNCER
They swing: the wing dips:
There's the signal: the dip: they'll
Dive: they're ready to dive:
They're steady: they're heading down:
They're dead on the town: they're nosing:
They're easing over: they're over:
There they go: there they—
>*(A crazy stammering of machine guns hammers above the rising roar.)*

A WOMAN'S VOICE *(shrieking)*
It's us do you see!

A WOMAN'S VOICE *(shrieking)*
>It's us don't you see us!

>*(For an instant the shrieking voices of the women, the shattering noise of the guns and the huge scream of the planes are mingled, then the voices are gone and the guns are gone and the scream of the planes closes to a deep sustained music note level and long as silence. After a moment comes the Boy's voice rising on each word, breaking off.)*

THE BOY'S VOICE
Harry! Harry! Harry! . . .
>*(The diminishing music note again—level—long.)*

[149]

THE VOICE OF THE YOUNG MAN

Stay as you are: do not move:

Do not ever move . . .

> (*The diminishing music note again. Over it the voice
> of the Singing Woman rising in a slow screaming scale
> of the purest agony broken at last on the unbearably
> highest note. The diminishing drone of the planes fades
> into actual silence.*)

PRELUDE TO APOCALYPSE
by André Malraux

TOLEDO

Above the clouds the air was marvellously clear. An infinite peace brooded upon the white sea of clouds under the plane, and there was as yet no sign of enemy air-patrols moving towards the city. According to the pilot's reckoning they were quite near Toledo. The plane accelerated to its maximum speed. Jaime was singing, the others straining to see ahead, with the fixed stare of absent-mindedness. In the distance some isolated mountain peaks pierced the level whiteness of the cloud-floor, and sometimes through a rift they had a glimpse of cornfields.

By now the machine was presumably above Toledo. But there was no instrument to record the drift due to a wind blowing directly at right angles to their course. Once the plane came down through the clouds it was almost certain to be spotted from the town and, if they were too far from it, the enemy pursuit planes would be on them before they had had time to drop their bombs. The plane swooped down.

Expecting every moment to catch sight of the earth below, of the guns of the Alcazar, the enemy pursuit planes and his lines of defense, Marcelino and the pilot watched the height-gauge more passionately than they had ever scanned a human face. 2500 . . . 1800 . . . 1200 feet. . . . But still they were immersed in clouds. There was no choice but to climb back, and wait till a hole appeared below them.

They zoomed into the upper air poised motionless above the clouds that seemed to stream away beneath them, following the earth's movement. The wind was driving the cloud-bank from east to west, and here it was pocked with numerous holes. They began to circle, with the immutable precision of a star, in the empty firmament. Jaime, who was in charge of the forward machine-gun, waved his hand to Marcelino.

For the first time both men grew conscious of the earth's rotation. An unheeded atom in the vast cosmic movement, the aeroplane gyrated like a tiny planet, waiting till the old city, the rebel Alcazar and its besiegers came into view below, rolled round in the incessant rhythm of earthbound things.

But at the first rift in the clouds—too small for observation—the instinct of the bird of prey came uppermost again. Like a circling hawk the plane swung round and round, prospecting for a larger opening, the gaze of all on board set vigilantly earthwards. It seemed to them that they themselves were stationary and the clouds and peaks were wheeling slowly round them on a far-flung orbit. Suddenly, at the fringe of a cloud-rift, the earth came into view, and two hundred yards or so away a little puff-ball floated past; the Alcazar had opened fire. The machine swooped again.

Space seemed to contract and the bright air faded out as the plane dived below the clouds. Here was man's little world. The Alcazar.

Toledo was on the left and, at the angle of their descent, the gorge above the Tagus loomed larger than the city, than the Alcazar itself, which was still firing up at them. The gun-layers were officers in the Artillery School, but the real danger for the crew lay in the enemy's pursuit planes rather than in gun-fire from below.

Slanting at first, Toledo was swinging slowly back to the horizontal. Even at this strange moment it had not lost its quaintly decorative air, and the expanse of roofs was striped with ribbons of smoke from burning houses. The plane began to circle, at a tangent to the Alcazar. This hawk-like circling above their quarry was imperative. The besieging troops were so close to the Alcazar that each bomb had to be dropped with absolute accuracy on the target. But each successive circle gave the enemy more time to bring up their pursuit planes. Marcelino's machine had come down to nine hundred feet and now he saw below him ant-like forms with round white hats, moving in front of the Alcazar.

The first time over, Marcelino opened the trap, took his sight without loosing off the bomb, and checked up on it. The sight was a good one, as he could judge. The Alcazar was a small target, and fearing the scatter effect of light bombs, he decided to use heavy ones only. He had withheld the signal, and the rest of the crew stood by, waiting. A second time the cockpit telegraph told the pilot to turn. The puff-balls of smoke were coming closer.

"Stand by!" Marcelino shouted.

Standing up in the cabin, with his beltless overalls flopping round him as usual, Marcelino was an ungainly figure. He never let the Alcazar out of his sight. He pulled the trap-hatch wide open and squatted down. A gust of cold air swept up the cabin and all of them knew the fight was going to begin.

The Alcazar veered again, approached. Now Marcelino was lying flat on his stomach, his wrist in air, counting the seconds. Then his arm fell as if it were ripping down a curtain. The Alcazar swept underneath, with a few ill-aimed shells circling it like satellites, spun round and sheered off to the right.

A tenuous puff of smoke appeared in the main courtyard; was it the bomb? The pilot continued to wheel round, taking the Alcazar again at a tangent. The bomb had fallen in the middle of the courtyard. Followed by bursts of shrapnel, the plane dropped a second bomb, swerved off, returned. Marcelino raised his hand again, but this time did not let it fall. In the courtyard white sheets had been hastily spread out; the Alcazar was surrendering!

THE BOMBING OF TALAVERA

The war had resolved itself into an endless succession of night-flights in machines endlessly repaired.

The plane took off; rose through the clouds.

"Say, young man?"

"Well?"

"Take a look at me. I may spend all my time fooling round. But I'm a man!"

He did not like Attignies, but every airman on active service respected courage, and Attignies' courage was beyond question. They went beneath the clouds again.

Listening to the reassuring yet constantly precarious throbbing of the engine, with his grey cloak over his head, Leclerc's feeling of godlike freedom took him back to the Great War, back to China; it was a freedom greater than sleep and war, greater than pain and passion.

A pause. Then, in the tone of a decision following ripe reflection, Leclerc said:

"You are a man, too."

Attignies did not want to hurt the pilot's feelings, but this kind of conversation got on his nerves. He grunted by way of answer, without lifting his eyes from the Milky Way etched in lights along the road beneath him; watching it streaming into the darkness in front of them, trembling in a wind they could not feel above, Attignies felt a desperate friendliness for that one sign of human life amid the dark, threatening, hostile solitude. There was no other light; to fall meant death. And as if some instinct more receptive than his conscious mind had forestalled his ears, Attignies suddenly perceived the reason for his feeling of distress: the engine was knocking.

"A valve!" he shouted to Leclerc.

"To hell with it!" the other shouted back. "We can take a chance."

Attignies tightened the strap of his crash-helmet; he was always ready to take a chance.

Talavera appeared on the horizon, magnified by its isolation amid the darkness. Level with the hills, its lights merged with the stars; they seemed to be coming forward to meet the plane. The stutter of the engine invested the town with an ominous reality. Amid the normal lights of a provincial town and the fretful, restless gleams that betokened military activity, the black patch indicating the darkened gas-works had something of the tense repose of a sleeping wild animal. Now the plane was flying over a tarred road, the wet surface of which reflected the light of the gas street-lamps after the recent rain. The mass of lights expanded steadily as the plane approached Talavera, and suddenly Attignies saw them from both windows at once as the old machine dived, like stars round a climbing plane.

He opened the improvised trap-door: the cold night air rushed into the cabin. On his knees up above the town, he waited, his field of vision limited by the bomb-sight like a horse in blinkers. Heading straight for the square black mass of the gas-works, his ears pricked up, Leclerc was bearing down upon the skeleton of light that was Talavera.

He swept over the black patch and turned round in a fury upon Attignies, of whom he could see nothing but his fair hair, gleaming faintly in the half-light inside the machine.

"What the hell are you doing?"

"Shut your choke!"

Leclerc tilted the plane sideways; still under the influence of the speed of the plane, the falling bombs were accompanying them, a little below them and a little behind, shining like fish in the moonlight. As pigeons veering in the air narrow into thin silhouettes, the bombs suddenly faded from their sight; their fall was becoming vertical. Close beside the gas-works a row of red explosions sprang into view.

"Missed."

Leclerc turned sharply and came back over the objective, going still lower. "Watch the height!" Attignies shouted; the change of height would alter the deflection. He looked at the altimeter, and then through the trap-door again. Seen from the opposite direction now, Talavera had changed in appearance like a man who turns round: the confused light thrown upon the streets from the military staff offices had given place to the lighted rectangles of the windows. The outline of the gas-works was less clear. The machine-guns were firing down below, but it was unlikely that the men handling them could see the plane distinctly. Every light in the town went out leaving the illuminated dashboard and the shadow of Leclerc's cloak upon the dial of the altimeter the sole things visible against the starlit sky.

Its far-flung lights had given the town a vague semblance of life, and the sharply defined lights revealed by the plane's return journey had suggested something still more precise; but now that it was in darkness the town really came into being. Like sparks struck from a flint, the short flames of the machine-guns appeared and disappeared. The enemy town was on the watch, seeming to move in response to each movement of the returning plane, in which Leclerc was staring fixedly, two wisps of hair protruding from the grey cloak covering his head. Attignies was flat on his stomach, eyes glued to his sight, through which the smallest bend in the river was coming into view, mist-blue in the moonlight: the gas-works came into view. He released the second rack of bombs.

They did not see them as they fell this time. The plane nose-dived to the accompaniment of a stupendous crash, and underneath there was a sudden burst of lightning-colored fire. To escape the blue flames surging up around them, Leclerc tugged frantically at the stick: the plane zoomed up towards the impassive serenity of the stars; below, there was nothing but a seething mass of red flames—the gas-works had been blown up.

Bullets drove through the fuselage. Perhaps the explosion had disclosed the position of the plane; a machine-gun was following its outline as it entered the halo around the moon. Leclerc began to zig-zag. Turning round, Attignies saw that a network of red flames was spreading out below. The stick of bombs had also hit the barracks close beside the gas-works.

A cloud-bank hid the ground from them.

Leclerc picked up the thermos flask beside him, then stopped in amazement, holding the cup in the air, and signing to Attignies; the whole plane was phosphorescent, glowing with a bluish light. Attignies pointed to the sky. Till then they had been looking to the ground, engrossed in their raid, and had not noticed the plane itself; above and behind them the moon, which they could not see, was lighting up the aluminum on the wings. Leclerc put the thermos down; what human gesture would not have seemed trivial and inadequate? Taking them far away from their instrument-board—the only visible light in all the waste of air around them—that sense of well-being which follows on all physical conflict was merging into an almost geological tranquillity, incorporating them in the mystic union of moonlight and pale metal gleaming as precious stones have gleamed for countless ages on the extinct stars. The shadow of the plane moved steadily over the cloud beneath them. Leclerc raised his forefinger, grimaced in approbation, and shouted gravely: "Something to remember, eh!" Picking up the thermos again, he noticed that the engine was still knocking.

THE NIGHT OF NOVEMBER 6TH

Three of the bombers had been repaired. Magnin's plane, known as the "Jaurès," was flying over the sleeping Balearics. For the last hour it had been alone above the sea. Attignies was piloting. All around the badly extinguished lights of Palma, the anti-aircraft guns were spitting up shells against the invisible plane; the town below was defending itself like a blind man screaming. Magnin was looking for a Nationalist cruiser and the ships loaded with arms in the harbor. Searchlights were stabbing through the darkness behind and in front of him, intersecting each other. He thought tensely that it was like using thin wands to catch a fly. Except for the pilot's cabin, the bomber was in complete darkness.

Were they fighting against an enemy or against cold? It was more than eighteen degrees below freezing point. The gunners detested having to fire with their gloves on, but in the intense cold to touch the metal of the guns meant burns. The bombs threw up spouts of water into the night, lighting them with an orange glow. They would have to find out from the War Ministry whether the ships had been hit.

Each one of them was watching the anti-aircraft shells burst around him. With ice-cold faces and bodies enclosed in the warmth of their fur-lined flying-suits, they were alone in the vast darkness stretching over the sea.

The plane suddenly lit up.

"For Christ's sake, put that out!" Magnin shouted. But the

very next moment he saw the shadows of the plane's wings, and realized that the light had come from outside.

The searchlight returned, catching the plane again. Magnin saw Pol's good-humored face and Gardet's back with the little rifle slung across it. They had carried out the bombing in complete darkness, broken by the blue lightnings of the anti-aircraft shells they had so far avoided. It was their comradeship in arms that had brought them into that cabin filled with menacing light; for the first time since they began their flight, these men could *see each other*.

One and all were peering down at the searchlight to which that blinding beam linked them. They all knew that focussing itself along that same line there was a gun.

Down below lights were going out, pursuit planes were no doubt taking off and the darkness stretched away to the horizon. And in the midst of darkness, with the plane shaking them about like shot in a box as it spun earthwards in an unsuccessful attempt to free itself from the searchlight, were those seven men bathed in blue effulgence.

Magnin sprang to the side of Attignies, who was tugging at the stick, his eyes closed to escape from that blinding dazzle. Three seconds more and the anti-aircraft guns would have opened fire.

The left hand of every occupant of the cabin went to the buckle of his parachute.

Attignies banked, teeth clenched and feet tensed against the controls, wishing with every fibre of his body, from his toes upwards, that he were in a pursuit plane; the bomber was turning with the unwieldiness of a lorry. And the light was still after them.

The first shell—thirty yards away. The plane jolted violently.

The anti-aircraft guns would correct the error. Magnin tore aside the ear-flap of Attignies' flying-helmet.

"Falling-leaf," the pilot shouted, indicating the manoeuvre with his hand.

It was the device by which a plane frees itself from a hurricane when the controls no longer function: a pendulum with all the weight of the machine behind it.

Magnin's moustache registered a frantic protest, visible but inaudible in the white glare and the noise of the engines. The searchlight would follow their swings down. He made another movement indicating a sideslip, followed by a turn.

Attignies went into a skid that seemed like a fall, with a noise of clanking metal and cartridge-clips rolling about the cabin. He fell headlong into an abyss of darkness, turned and made off in a corkscrew curve. Above and below the searchlight went stabbing through the sky like a blind man feeling his way with a rapier.

The plane was well clear of the searchlight zone now—lost once more in the protecting night. As if sinking into the repose of sleep, the crew of the plane had regained their posts and were luxuriating in the relief which was the invariable sequel to an engagement; driving through the freezing darkness above a lightless sea. But each of them had vividly before him the picture of the features of his comrades as they had been thrown into relief for that brief moment.

CRASH

Bleeding, but not badly hit, Pujol could feel the contact of the stick welded to his body, identified with it, as the others felt their wounds. The counter dropped from 1,200 to 1,100.

Underneath them lay the spurs of the snow mountain. Landing there meant plunging headlong into the ravines, like a drunken wasp dashing itself to pieces against a wall. A broad undulating expanse of snow lay beyond. And what underneath?

They went into a cloud, a zone of snowy whiteness; the floor of the fuselage was patterned with red footprints. Pujol was trying to rise above the cloud. Actually their unchecked fall brought them out below it. They were only 60 yards from the mountain. The earth was rushing towards them; how would these soft curves treat them . . . ? They wanted desperately to come through alive, now that they had brought off the bombing successfully and escaped the machine-guns.

"The bomb!" Gardet shouted.

If it failed to dislodge itself this time, they would all be blown sky high. Saïdi wrenched at both handles of the releasing mechanism, tugging them frantically downwards. The bomb fell, and the snow engulfed them as though the earth had been flung up against the plane by its fall.

Pujol sprang from his seat, suddenly open to the sky. Deaf? No, it must be the silence of the mountains after the noise of the crash, for he could hear a crow cawing, the shouts. Blood was trickling gently down his face and punching red holes in the snow in front of his shoes. His cheeks felt warm. He had nothing but his hands with which to wipe away the blood that was blinding him—through which he had a confused view of a black heap of metal loud with cries; the fantastic, inextricably fused tangle characteristic of wrecked aeroplanes.

PART VII

Remember This Machine

To Poets and Airmen
by Stephen Spender

Thinkers and airmen—all such
    Friends and pilots upon the edge
Of the skies of the future—much
    You require a bullet's eye of courage
    To fly through this age.

The paper brows are winged and helmeted,
    The blind ankles bound to a white road,
Which streams into a night of lead
    Where cities explode.
    Fates unload

Hatred burning, in small parcels,
    Outrage against social lies,
Hearts breaking against stone refusals
    Of men to show small mercies
    To men. Now death replies
Releasing new, familiar devils.

And yet, before you throw away your childhood
    With the lambs pasturing in flaxen hair,
    To plunge into this iron war,
Remember for a flash the wild good
    Drunkenness where
    You abandoned future care.

And then forget. Become what
  Things require. The expletive word.
  The all-night-long screeching metal bird.
And all of time shut down in one shot
  Of night by a gun uttered.

For the joy that was is hidden under grass,
  Shadows of hawks flicker over.
Buried in cellars is laughter that once was
  Which the pick and shovel endeavor
  Vainly to uncover;
Like a child buried when the raiders pass.

With axe and shovel men hunt among the bricks,
  With lamps and water, for their soul
Of lilac in the city square; they hack with picks
  Amongst the ruins for their love's goal,
  As though a smile frozen at the North Pole
Might take pity on their tricks.

London, December, 1940

A Letter to Robert Graves
by T. E. Lawrence

4.2.35   *Ozone Hotel, Bridlington*

New page, new subject . . . I feel that the Middle Eastern settlement put through by Winston Churchill and Young and me in 1921 (which stands in every particular . . . if only the other Peace Treaties did!) should weigh more than fighting. And I feel too that this settlement should weigh less than my life since 1922, for the conquest of the last element, the air, seems to me the only major task of our generation; and I have convinced myself that progress today is made not by the single genius, but by the common effort. To me it is the multitude of rough transport drivers, filling all the roads of England every night, who make this the mechanical age. And it is the airmen, the mechanics, who are overcoming the air, not the Mollisons and Orlebars. The genius raids, but the common people occupy and possess. Wherefore I stayed in the ranks and served to the best of my ability, much influencing my fellow airmen towards a pride in themselves and their inarticulate duty. I tried to make them see—with some success.

That for eight years, and now for the last four I have been so curiously fortunate as to share in a little revolution we have made in boat design. People have thought we were at finality there, for since 1850 ships have merely got bigger. When I went into R.A.F. boats in 1929, every type was an Admiralty design. All were round-bottomed, derived from the first hollow tree, with only a fin, called a keel, to delay their rolling about and over. They progressed by pushing their own bulk of water aside. Now (1935) not one type of R.A.F. boat in production is naval. . . . We have found, chosen, selected or derived our own sorts: they have (power for power) three times the speed of their predecessors, less weight, less cost, more room, more safety, more seaworthiness. As their speed increases, they rise out of the water and run over its face. They cannot roll, nor pitch, having no pendulum nor period, but a subtly modelled planing bottom and sharp edges.

Now I do not claim to have made these boats. They have grown out of the joint experience, skill and imaginations of many men. But I can (secretly) feel that they owe to me their opportunity and their acceptance. The pundits met them with a fierce hostility: all the R.A.F. sailors, and all the Navy, said that they would break, sink, wear out, be unmanageable. Today we are advising the War Office in refitting the coast defences entirely with boats of our model, and the Admiralty has specified them for the modernized battleships: while the German, Chinese, Spanish and Portuguese Governments have adopted them! In inventing them we have had to make new engines, new auxiliaries, use new timbers, new metals, new materials. It has been five years of intense and co-ordinated progress. Nothing now hinders the application of our design to big ships—except the conservatism of man, of course. Patience. It cannot be stopped now.

All this boasting is not to glorify myself, but to explain; and here enters my last subject for this letter, your strictures upon the changes I have made in myself since the time we felt so much together at Oxford. You're quite right about the change. I was then trying to write; to be perhaps an artist (for *The Seven Pillars* had pretensions towards design, and was written with great pains as prose) or to be at least cerebral. My head was aiming to create intangible things. That's not well put: all creation is tangible. What I was trying to do, I suppose, was to carry a superstructure of ideas upon or above anything I made.

Well, I failed in that. By measuring myself against such people as yourself and Augustus John, I could feel that I was not made out of the same stuff. Artists excite and attract me, seduce me, from what I am. Almost I could be an artist, but there is a core that puts on the brake. If I knew what it was I would tell you. Only I can't.

So I changed direction, right, and went into the R.A.F. after straightening out that Eastern tangle with Winston, a duty that fell to me, I having been partly the cause of the tangle. How well the Middle East has done: it, more than any part of the world, has gained from that war.

However, as I said, I went into the R.A.F. to serve a mechanical purpose, not as leader but as a cog of the machine. I have been mechanical since, and a good mechanic, for my self-training as an artist has greatly widened my field of view. I leave it to others to say whether I chose well or not: one of the benefits of being part of the machine is that one learns that one doesn't matter!

One thing more. You remember me writing to you when I first went into the R.A.F. that it was the nearest modern equivalent of going into a monastery in the Middle Ages. That was right in more than one sense. Being a mechanic cuts one off from all real communication with women. There are no women in the machines, in any machine. No woman, I believe, can understand a mechanic's happiness in serving his bits and pieces. . . . Don't worry or regret or desire me to change the face of nature. We are lucky to have proportion and toleration to pad our bones.

Yours

T. E. S.

[169]

THE STORY OF MY DEATH
by Lauro de Bosis

Tomorrow at three o'clock, in a meadow on the Côte d'Azur, I have a rendezvous with Pegasus.

Pegasus is the name of my aeroplane. It has a russet body and white wings; and though it is as strong as eighty horses, it is as slim as a swallow. Drunk with petrol, it leaps through the sky like its brother of old, but in the night it can glide at will through the air like a phantom. I found it in the Hercynian forest, and its old master will bring it to me on the shores of the Tyrrhenian Sea, believing in perfect sincerity that it will serve the pleasures of an idle young Englishman. My bad accent has not awakened his suspicions; I hope he will pardon my subterfuge.

And yet we are not going in search of chimeras, but to bear a message of liberty across the sea to a people that is in chains. To drop figures of speech (which I had to use to leave the origins of my aeroplane discreetly vague) we are going to Rome to scatter from the air these words of liberty which, for seven years, have been forbidden like a crime. And with reason, for if they had been allowed they would have shaken the Fascist tyranny to its foundations within a few hours.

Every regime in the world, even the Afghan and the Turkish, allows its subjects a certain amount of liberty. Fascism alone, in self-defense, is obliged to annihilate thought. It cannot be blamed for punishing faith in liberty, and fidelity to the Italian Constitution more severely than parricide: that is its only chance of existence. It cannot be blamed for deporting thousands of citizens without trial, or for meting out several thousand years of imprisonment in the space of four years. How could it dominate a free people if it did not terrorize them with its garrison of three hundred thousand mercenaries? Fascism has no choice. If one shares its point of view, one is obliged to declare with its apostle Mussolini: "Liberty is a rotten carcass." If one merely wishes it to last, one must approve the murder of Matteotti and the rewards meted out to his murderers, the destruction of all the newspapers of Italy, the sacking of the house of Croce, the millions spent on espionage and on *agents provocateurs,* in short, the sword of Damocles suspended over the head of every citizen.

In June 1930 I started to put in circulation bi-monthly letters, of a strictly constitutional character, explaining the necessity that all men of law and order should be in accord in preparation for the day when Fascism should fall. Since Fascism seems to have adopted the motto "after us the deluge," the initiative was more opportune, and as a matter of fact, the letters, according to the principle of the snowball, began to circulate by thousands. For five months I carried on the work alone, sending every fortnight six hundred letters signed "National Alliance," with the request that each recipient should send on six copies. Unfortunately, in December, during a short voyage which I was obliged to make abroad, the police arrested the two friends who had agreed to post the letters during my absence. They were subjected to torture and condemned to fifteen years' imprisonment. One of them, Mario Vinciguerra, one of the best-known writers of Italy, literary and art critic, although he was not well at the time, was left all night entirely naked (it was a night in December) on the roof of police head-quarters in Rome. As a result of repeated blows on the head he has remained completely deaf in one ear.

He was thrown into a cell six feet square, where there was not even a chair to sit on, and from which every morning his bed was removed. After the protest of foreign papers and of eminent political personages, both English and American, his conditions were bettered. Mussolini even went so far as to offer their liberty to both men if they would write a letter of submission, but this they refused to do.

The day on which I read of the arrest of my friends, I was on the point of crossing the frontier to return to Italy. My first instinct, naturally, was to go to Rome to share their fate, but I realized that the duty of a soldier is not to surrender, but to fight to the end. I decided immediately to go to Rome, not in order to surrender, but to carry on the work of the National Alliance by throwing four hundred thousand letters from the air, and then, either to fall in fighting or return to my base to make other plans. The sky of Rome had never been flown by enemy aeroplanes. I shall be the first—I said to myself—and I began at once to prepare the expedition. The venture was not an easy one, because for a poet it is always difficult even to earn his daily bread, and if he is exiled besides, and to cap the climax in a year of crisis, it is not surprising if he quickly descends to the lowest degrees of a Bohemian life. And then, I did not even know how to drive a motorcycle, not to mention an aeroplane! I began by finding employment as a *concierge* at the Hotel Victor Emmanuel III, rue de Ponthieu. My republican friends said that I was rightly punished there where I had sinned! To tell the truth I was not only *concierge* but also book-keeper and telephone operator. Often three or four bells would ring at the same time, and I would cry up the stairs in a stentorian voice, "Irma, two portions of butter for number 35!" As a preparation for my raid over Rome it was not very effective. However, between the baker's bills and the clients' receipts, I was writing a message to the King of Italy and studying a map of the Tyrrhenian Sea. The rest of my preparation is the most interesting part of the story, but unfortunately it must remain secret.

In May I made my first solo flight in a Farman machine near Versailles. Then, having heard that my secret had reached the ears of the Fascists, I disappeared, and appeared again under a different name in England. On July 13th I left Cannes in an English biplane, carrying with me eighty kilos of tracts. As I had done only five hours of solo flying I went alone so as not to risk the life of a friend. Unfortunately an accident on the coast of Corsica ended my venture, and I had to escape, leaving my aeroplane in a field. My secret was now revealed. In Italy they had no difficulty in realizing who the mysterious pilot was. The English and French police began a search for me with a diligence that flattered me; they even disputed my portrait. I ask their pardon for the trouble that I have caused them.

The worst of it was that I could now no more rely on the surprise, my greatest chance of success. None the less, Rome became for me as Cape Horn to the Flying Dutchman: dead or alive I swore to get there. My death—however undesired by me personally, who have so many things to achieve—could not but add to the success of my flight. As all the dangers lie on the return flight, I shall not die until I have delivered my four hundred thousand letters, which will only be the better *recommandées!* After all, it is the question of giving a small example of civic spirit, and to draw the attention of my fellow citizens to their real situation. I am convinced that Fascism will not end until some twenty young people sacrifice their lives in order to awaken the spirit of the Italians. While during the Risorgimento there were thousands of young men who were ready to give their lives, today there are very few. Why? It is not that their courage and their faith are less than that of their fathers. It is because no one takes Fascism seriously. Beginning with its leaders, everyone counts on its speedy fall, and it seems out of proportion to give one's life to end something that will collapse by itself. That is a mistake. It is necessary to die. I hope that many others will follow me and will at last succeed in arousing public opinion.

Besides my letters, I shall throw down several copies of a splendid book by Bolton King, *Fascism in Italy*. As one throws bread on a starving city, one must throw history books on Rome.

After having flown over Corsica and the Island of Monte Cristo at a height of twelve thousand feet, I shall reach Rome about eight o'clock, having done the last twenty kilometres gliding. Though I have only done seven and a half hours solo flying, if I fall it will not be through fault of pilotage. My aeroplane only flies at 150 kilometres an hour, whereas those of Mussolini can do 300. There are nine hundred of them and they have all received the order to bring down at any cost, with machine-gun fire, any suspicious aeroplane. However little they may know me, they must realize that after my first attempt I have not given up. If my friend Balbo has done his duty, they are there waiting for me. So much the better; I shall be worth more dead than alive.

October 2, 1931

Elegy on the Pilot
by Reuel Denney

Death in an ancient country was a simple passport
To heights so Himalaya-like the ghost itself was frozen
Like a god's breath, blown out in winter sleeping,
Contracted on death's hill so small a pin could pierce a million.
Yet some in an uncorporeal fire as fierce as oil's and whiter,
Were bathed so softly that they sang as bones were turned to
    snow.
Death in some countries was a fine felucca, freighted,
And a man with a dog face at the helm, who knew the way
    to go.
On various tongues life veered to various ends;
Some misers ended spiders, and spiders ended kings;
And whether all flowed or stayed, each to the scheme sank back
As molecules, majestic in the wave, serve springs.

Skies that they saw in death, this pilot saw awake:
Unsmoky stars in animals that, pricked on the tented spaces,
Swung the great circus of the year not with platonic music
But the silence of machinery too far to hear or guess.
Above eight thousand feet his prow's blunt sucking silver
Burst through the veil of fog like a whale through silver schools,
And, plumed with corkscrew ribbons of that mist,
Drifted such lunar distances as Arctic breathes and cools.
His hand moved with the dials: his polished power fled

Through the vast court of midnight like a prayer's wan word
Whose syllable, in the shrine, flies whispering down the floor
Toward the carved ear, unseen, of an awakened god.

Call all the birds of Audubon
Out of the south, and here upon
The birdman's snowy mound let them
Lay blooms and berries fresh of stem.
Let them bring moss the lowland grows
On oaks where slow Savannah flows,
And acid fruits of juniper,
And acorns, and the chestnut flower,
And pickerel weed from brooks of Maine,
And a pine's silver-dusted cone.
Each state will yield a separate bloom
To garland up his noiseless tomb
And keep some recollection of
These provinces he flew above.
These petals, taken as they were,
From summer pastures' pleasant whirr,
Or in the inaccessible flow
Of streams whose blue is only snow,
Will speak what sorrows, undefined,
Rest in the earth, or in the mind.
Bright, unpremeditated there
As in uncertain April air
A violet opens in surprise
Its cold and ferny-lidded eyes
To form, when centuries are gone,
The tint with which it first began,
These perfectly inhuman things
Will sing when mind no longer sings

The sorrow of gone competence,
The ruin and the violence.
Their tenderness is such a lie,
Concealing, like the gardened way
Of Florida from de Leon,
The death the search of youth has gone;
Misrepresenting savagery
Like that high-blooming tulip tree
Which, taller than the woods around,
Drew men to dark and bloody ground,
That all the innocence of years
May end, and ending turn to tears.

A few young men go off and from the air
Sweep creek and jungle with a camera's eye.
The map's a map to them, and misty there
The archipelagoes drift by.
The continents loom up, they trail the ranges,
Land on the snows and lift like cranes from waters;
In crevices of cloud they breathe the changes
Of upper climates in ascending layers.
They hunt sequestered and unclever men
And land their laughing hopes on ponds unknown.

At home the raging system that allows
A few their conversation in the clouds
Keeps thousands ready for the brief repairs
And warms them with what fables are allowed.
They also in the mist can feel the mountains
Claw close, as they pass by them in their speed;
The air drops out, their wings are also tatters;
They scream and fall and grass rubs out the deed.

The freedom of a few is such a flame
It burns a mob to make one glittering name.
Because all tools are in the end one tool,
Because all wings are in the end one bird,
Was every raving democrat a fool
And will the tyrants have the final word?
The flight was well begun, the navigation
Made more than one companion to the stars,
And each heroic expectation
Flew fresher from the doubtful wars.
Or are they dreams the fist lets go like sand,
That the people made, but did not understand?

DARK

by Anne Morrow Lindbergh

"What time does it get dark at Nome?" My husband pushed a penciled message back to me. Dark? I had completely forgotten that it ever was dark. We had been flying in the land of the midnight sun, though actually its period was over in August. The sun set, but the sky did not darken on either of the flights, from Baker Lake to Aklavik, or from Aklavik to Barrow. But tonight—for it was about eight-thirty in the evening—the light was fading rather fast. Streaks of the remaining sunset ran gold in the inlets and lagoons of the coast. We had turned the corner of Alaska after leaving Point Barrow and were flying south to the little mining town, Nome, on the Bering coast. An unknown route, an unknown harbor; we must have light to land.

"WXB—WXB—WXB," I called back to our friend at the Barrow radio station. I had tried in vain to reach Nome. "Nil—hrd (nothing heard)—from—WXY (Nome)—or—WXW (Kotzebue)—what—time—does—it—get—dark—at—Nome?" His faint signals traced dim incomprehensible marks on my brain, then faded away. It was no use; I could not make them out. I would have to let go of that thread and pick up another.

"Can't—copy—ur (your)—sigs (signals)—will—contact—NRUL (the *Northland*)." I signed off. There was no time to lose. Again I tried, "NRUL—de—KHCL—nil—hrd—from—WXY—what—time—does—it—get—dark—at—Nome?" No answer. The sparks from the exhaust flashed behind us in the growing dusk.

Was it really going to get dark? It had not been dark since Baker Lake, since that evening when we set out recklessly at seven to fly all night. It had seemed, I remembered, a kind of madness to start at that hour. It would soon be dark, or so I thought, and to fly at night, in a strange country, through uncertain weather to an unknown destination—what were we thinking of! Spendthrifts with daylight, we who usually count every coin; who always rose early to fly, at three or four in the morning, not to waste a second of the precious light; we were down at the field, the engine warmed up and ready to start with the first streaks of dawn, in order to "get there by dark." Dark— that curfew hour in a flier's mind, when the gates are closed, the portcullis dropped down, and there is no way to go around or to squeeze under the bars if one is late.

But that night at Baker Lake, we were going north, into the land of the midnight sun. "And it will be light all the way?" we had asked incredulously. (Though of course we knew it to be so.)

"Sure—it won't get dark at all—going north like that." The game warden had nodded his head. "Light all the way!"

Going into that strange world of unending day was like stepping very quietly across the invisible border of the land of Faery that the Irish poets write of, that timeless world of Fionn and Saeve, or the world of Thomas the Rhymer. It was evening when we left Baker Lake, but an evening that would never flower into night, never grow any older. And so we had set out, released from fear, intoxicated with a new sense of freedom— out into that clear unbounded sea of day. We could go on and on and never reach the shores of night. The sun would set, darkness would gather in the bare coves, creep over the waste lands behind us, but never overtake us. The wave of night would draw itself together, would rise behind us and never break.

But now—going south— My husband switched on the instrument lights. We were running short of fuel. Our gasoline barrels were on the icebound *Northland* and we had not refueled since Aklavik. There was no chance of turning back. We must land before dark.

"NRUL—NRUL—what—time—does—it—get—dark—at—Nome?"

At Barrow, I remembered, we had even wanted the dark. When I went to bed the first night, I had pulled down the shades, trying to create the feeling of a deep black night. For sleep, one needs endless depths of blackness to sink into; daylight is too shallow, it will never cover one. At Aklavik, too, I had missed night's punctuality. It was light when we went to bed and light when we rose. The same light shed over breakfast and lunch and supper and continued on through bedtime, so that I hardly knew when to feel tired or when to feel hungry.

But now, seeing signs of approaching night—the coves and lagoons took up the light the sky was losing—I was afraid. I felt the terror of a savage seeing a first eclipse, or even as if I had never known night. What was it? Explorer from another planet, I watched with fear, with amazement, and with curiosity, as Emily Dickinson watched for day. . . . "Feathers like a bird," perhaps, answered my own questioning. The shadow of a wing covered all the sky. We would be covered, inclosed, crushed. Wisps of evening fog below grew luminous in the approaching dark. I remembered now what night was. It was being blind and lost and trapped. It was looking and not seeing—that was night.

"WXY—WXY—WXY—what—time—does—it—get—dark—at—Nome?"

Suddenly an answer: "WXN—WXN—Candle—Candle—" One of the relay stations on the coast had heard us, "Will—stand—by—in—case—you—don't—get—WXY," came their message. At last someone to answer.

"What—time—does—it—get—dark—at—Nome?"

There was a silence while he relayed the message to Nome. I looked out and caught my breath. The sea and sky had merged. The dark had leaped up several steps behind me when my back was turned. I would have to keep my eye on him or he would sneak up like the child's game of steps. But the radio was buzzing. My head went down again.

"The—men—are—going—to—put—flares—on—the—Nome—River," came back the answer, "it's—overcast—and—getting—dark." Then, continuing, "When—u (you)—expect—arrive—so —they—no (know)—when—lite—flares?"

I passed my scribbled message forward. The lights blinked on in the front cockpit. I read by my own light the reply, "Arrive in about 1½ hours—don't lite flares until plane circles and blinks lites."

An hour and a half more! It would be night when we landed! Turned inland, we were over mountains now and there were peaks ahead. It was darker over the land than over the water. Valleys hoard darkness as coves hoard light. Reservoirs of darkness, all through the long day they guard what is left them from the night before; but now their cups were filling up, trembling at the brim, ready to spill over. The wave of night climbed up behind us; gathering strength from every crevice, it towered over us.

Suddenly my husband pulled the plane up into a stall, throttled the engine, and, in the stillness that followed, shouted back to me, "Tell him there's fog on the mountains ahead. We'll land for the night and come into Nome in the morning."

"All right, where are we?"

"Don't know exactly—northwest coast of Seward Peninsula."

Without switching on the light I started tapping rapidly, "WXN—WXN—WXN—fog—on—mountains—ahead—will—land—for—night—and—come—into—Nome—morning—position—northwest—coast—Seward—Peninsula," I repeated twice.

"Hurry up! Going to land," came a shout from the front cockpit. We were banking steeply.

No time to try again. No time to listen for reply. I did not know if they had received it, but we could not wait to circle again. We must land before that last thread of light had gone.

Down, down, down, the cold air whistling through the cowlings as we dived toward the lagoon. I must wind in the antenna before we hit the water. The muscles in my arms stiffened to soreness turning the wheel at top speed, as though I were reeling in a gigantic fish from the bottom of the sea. One more turn—*jiggle, snap,* the ball-weight clicked into place—all wound up, safe. Now—brace yourself for the landing. How *can* he see anything? Spank, spank, spank. There we go—I guess we're all right! But the ship shot on through the water—on and on. Must have landed "down wind." Now it eased up a little. There, I sighed with relief. We were taxiing toward that dark indistinct line ahead—a shore. About half a mile off my husband pulled back the throttle, idled the engine for a few seconds, then cut the switch. In the complete stillness that followed, he climbed out onto the pontoon.

"Think we'd better anchor here." He uncoiled the rope and threw out the anchor. Splash! There it stayed under about three feet of water with the rope floating on top. Heavens! Pretty shallow—thought we had more room than that. Well, we were anchored anyway. We were down—we were safe. Somewhere out on the wild coast of Seward Peninsula.

At Nome it was dark now. The bonfire that was to have welcomed us lit up an empty shore as the crowd straggled home. It was dark where we were on the coast of Seward Peninsula. A little light surprised us from the blackness miles away—a single Eskimo camp perhaps. We made a bed in the baggage compartment out of our parachutes, our flying suits, and sleeping bags, and stretched out. The wave of night broke over us and we slept.

THE TOOL

by Antoine de Saint Exupéry
(*Translated by Lewis Galantière*)

And now, having spoken of the men born of the pilot's craft, I shall say something about the tool with which they work—the airplane. Have you looked at a modern airplane? Have you followed from year to year the evolution of its lines? Have you ever thought, not only about the airplane but about whatever man builds, that all of man's industrial efforts, all his computations and calculations, all the nights spent over working draughts and blueprints, invariably culminate in the production of a thing whose sole and guiding principle is the ultimate principle of simplicity?

It is as if there were a natural law which ordained that to achieve this end, to refine the curve of a piece of furniture, or a ship's keel, or the fuselage of an airplane, until gradually it partakes of the elementary purity of the curve of a human breast or shoulder, there must be the experimentation of several generations of craftsmen. In anything at all, perfection is finally attained not when there is no longer anything to add, but when there is no longer anything to take away, when a body has been stripped down to its nakedness.

It results from this that perfection of invention touches hands with absence of invention, as if that line which the human eye will follow with effortless delight were a line that had not been invented but simply discovered, had in the beginning been hidden by nature and in the end been found by the engineer. There is an ancient myth about the image asleep in the block of marble until it is carefully disengaged by the sculptor. The sculptor must himself feel that he is not so much inventing or shaping the curve of breast or shoulder as delivering the image from its prison.

In this spirit do engineers, physicists concerned with thermodynamics, and the swarm of preoccupied draughtsmen tackle their work. In appearance, but only in appearance, they seem to be polishing surfaces and refining away angles, easing this joint or stabilizing that wing, rendering these parts invisible, so that in the end there is no longer a wing hooked to a framework but a form flawless in its perfection, completely disengaged from its matrix, a sort of spontaneous whole, its parts mysteriously fused together and resembling in their unity a poem.

Meanwhile, startling as it is that all visible evidence of invention should have been refined out of this instrument and that there should be delivered to us an object as natural as a pebble polished by the waves, it is equally wonderful that he who uses this instrument should be able to forget that it is a machine.

There was a time when a flier sat at the centre of a complicated works. Flight set us factory problems. The indicators that oscillated on the instrument panel warned us of a thousand dangers. But in the machine of today we forget that motors are whirring: the motor, finally, has come to fulfil its function, which is to whirr as a heart beats—and we give no thought to the beating of our heart. Thus, precisely because it is perfect the machine dissembles its own existence instead of forcing itself upon our notice.

And thus, also, the realities of nature resume their pride of place. It is not with metal that the pilot is in contact. Contrary to the vulgar illusion, it is thanks to the metal, and by virtue of it, that the pilot rediscovers nature. As I have already said, the machine does not isolate man from the great problems of nature but plunges him more deeply into them.

Numerous, nevertheless, are the moralists who have attacked the machine as the source of all the ills we bear, who, creating a fictitious dichotomy, have denounced the mechanical civilization as the enemy of the spiritual civilization.

If what they think were really so, then indeed we should really have to despair of man, for it would be futile to struggle against this new advancing chaos. The machine is certainly as irresistible in its advance as those virgin forests that encroach upon equatorial domains. A congeries of motives prevents us from blowing up our spinning mills and reviving the distaff. Gandhi had a try at this sort of revolution; he was as simple-minded as a child trying to empty the sea on the sand with the aid of a teacup.

It is hard for me to understand the language of these pseudo-dreamers. What is it makes them think that the ploughshare torn from the bowels of the earth by perforating machines, forged, tempered, and sharpened in the roar of modern industry, is nearer to man than any other tool of steel? By what sign do they recognize the inhumanity of the machine?

Have they ever really asked themselves this question? The central struggle of men has ever been to understand one another, to join together for the common weal. And it is this very thing that the machine helps them to do! It begins by annihilating time and space.

To me, in France, a friend speaks from America. The energy that brings me his voice is born of dammed-up waters a thousand miles from where he sits. The energy I burn up in listening to him is dispensed in the same instant by a lake formed in the River Yser which, four thousand miles from him and five hundred from me, melts like snow in the action of the turbines.

Transport of the mails, transport of the human voice, transport of flickering pictures—in this century as in others our highest accomplishments still have the single aim of bringing men together. Do our dreamers hold that the invention of writing, of printing, of the sailing ship, degraded the human spirit?

It seems to me that those who complain of man's progress confuse ends with means. True, that man who struggles in the unique hope of material gain will harvest nothing worth while. But how can anyone conceive that the machine is an end? It is a tool. As much a tool as is the plough. The microscope is a tool. What disservice do we do the life of the spirit when we analyze the universe through a tool created by the science of optics, or seek to bring together those who love one another and are parted in space?

"Agreed!" my dreamers will say, "but explain to us why it is that a decline in human values has accompanied the rise of the machine?" Oh, I miss the village with its crafts and its folk-songs as much as they do! The town fed by Hollywood seems to me, too, impoverished despite its electric street lamps. I quite agree that men lose their creative instincts when they are fed thus without raising a hand. And I can see that it is tempting to accuse industry of this evil.

But we lack perspective for the judgment of transformations that go so deep. What are the hundred years of the history of the machine compared with the two hundred thousand years of the history of man? It was only yesterday that we began to pitch our camp in this country of laboratories and power stations, that we took possession of this new, this still unfinished, house we live in. Everything round us is new and different—our concerns, our working habits, our relations with one another.

Our very psychology has been shaken to its foundations, to its most secret recesses. Our notions of separation, absence, distance, return, are reflections of a new set of realities, though the words themselves remain unchanged. To grasp the meaning of the world of today we use a language created to express the world of yesterday. The life of the past seems to us nearer our true natures, but only for the reason that it is nearer our language.

Every step on the road of progress takes us farther from habits which, as the life of man goes, we had only recently begun to acquire. We are in truth emigrants who have not yet founded our homeland. We Europeans have become again young peoples, without tradition or language of our own. We shall have to age somewhat before we are able to write the folksongs of a new epoch.

Young barbarians still marveling at our new toys—that is what we are. Why else should we race our planes, give prizes to those who fly highest, or fastest? We take no heed to ask ourselves why we race: the race itself is more important than the object.

And this holds true of other things than flying. For the colonial soldier who founds an empire, the meaning of life is conquest. He despises the colonist. But was not the very aim of his conquest the settling of this very colonist?

In the enthusiasm of our rapid mechanical conquests we have overlooked some things. We have perhaps driven men into the service of the machine, instead of building machinery for the service of man. But could anything be more natural? So long as we were engaged in conquest, our spirit was the spirit of conquerors. The time has now come when we must be colonists, must make this house habitable which is still without character.

Little by little the machine will become part of humanity. Read the history of the railways in France, and doubtless elsewhere too: they had all the trouble in the world to tame the people of our villages. The locomotive was an iron monster. Time had to pass before men forgot what it was made of. Mysteriously, life began to run through it, and now it is wrinkled and old. What is it today for the villager except a humble friend who calls every evening at six?

The sailing vessel was once a machine born of the calculations of engineers, yet it does not disturb our philosophers. The sloop took its place in the speech of men. There is a poetry of sailing as old as the world. There have always been seamen in recorded time. The man who assumes that there is an essential difference between the sloop and the airplane lacks historical perspective.

Every machine will gradually take on this patina and lose its identity in its function.

Air and water, and not machinery, are the concern of the hydroplane pilot about to take off. The motors are running free and the plane is already ploughing the surface of the sea. Under the dizzying whirl of the scythelike propellers, clusters of silvery water bloom and drown the flotation gear. The element smacks the sides of the hull with a sound like a gong, and the pilot can sense this tumult in the quivering of his body. He feels the ship charging itself with power as from second to second it picks up speed. He feels the development, in these fifteen tons of matter, of a maturity that is about to make flight possible. He closes his hands over the controls, and little by little in his bare palms he receives the gift of this power. The metal organs of the controls, progressively as this gift is made him, become the messengers of the power in his hands. And when his power is ripe, then, in a gesture gentler than the culling of a flower, the pilot severs the ship from the water and establishes it in the air.